# THESE BONES WILL LIVE

# THESE BONES *Will* LIVE

How the Holy Spirit Connects
the Body of Christ as One

by Odie Hill

*These Bones Will Live*
**Copyright © 2004 by Odie Hill**
All Rights Reserved.

All Scripture references are from the King James Version of the Bible.

All references to Greek words are taken from *Vine's Expository Dictionary of Old and New Testament Words*, published September 1996 by Nelson Reference and Electronic Publishing, Nashville, Tennessee.

McDougal Publishing is a ministry of The McDougal Foundation, Inc., a Maryland nonprofit corporation dedicated to spreading the Gospel of the Lord Jesus Christ to as many people as possible in the shortest time possible.

Published by:

McDougal Publishing
P.O. Box 3595
Hagerstown, MD 21742-3595
www.mcdougalpublishing.com

ISBN 1-58158-079-7

Printed in the United States of America
For Worldwide Distribution

# Acknowledgments

To everyone who encouraged me to write this book: Because of you, this book did not die in the birth canal.

To Prophetess Yvonne Watts: Thanks for being a mentor and a friend to me. You believed in me even when I found believing difficult.

To Patricia Bryant: Thanks for encouraging me to continue to write and finish the book. Your long hours of working with me and helping me put this book into print are deeply appreciated.

To my sons, Darren Hill and Michael Hill: Thanks for your love and encouragement.

# Contents

Introduction 9

1. Can These Bones Live? 15
2. Jesus Christ: The Seed of the Woman 27
3. Ye Are the Body 37
4. Oneness in Christ 41
5. Communion 45
6. Feeding the Multitudes 51
7. The Body Is Not One Member 57
8. Who Needs Whom? 63
9. Governing Body 73
10. Behold, the Bridegroom Cometh 93
11. A Gentile Bride 97
12. The Twelve Tribes of Israel 103

# Introduction

*Know ye not that ye are the temple of God, and that the Spirit of God dwelleth in you? If any man defile the temple of God, him shall God destroy; for the temple of God is holy, which temple ye are.*
1 Corinthians 3:16-17

God has created a Body of believers on earth to become His family. The seed of life is in this family, this Body, and we are to become a reflection of Him by once again reproducing righteousness on the earth.

The Body of Christ is interrelated and its members are connected one to another even as our physical body's organs and systems are interrelated and our bones are joined together. The systems in the body are designed to facilitate one another. The same is true of the Body of Christ.

God's plan for Christ's Body on earth is a unifying program of action that edifies and maintains the Body. The goal of this plan is to bring man back to God's original design with God's DNA as the unifying force, rather than the DNA of man that preserved him up until the coming of the Redeemer. In God's original design, man was joined to God. His root, or beginning, came from God.

God sent His Son, the Seed of the woman, to suffer the penalty for man's fall. Jesus suffered the baptism of death and resurrection that brought us into newness of life. His tomb became a womb for the birthing of the first prophetic word, given to Adam and Eve, that the Seed of the woman would bruise the serpent's head.

Jesus came to restore the original plan for man—to be a spiritual being made in the likeness and image of God. Sin and rebellion had caused man's image to become distorted, disjointed, and disconnected. Therefore, Jesus came to provide the solution. He was nailed to the cross for all of mankind, to be made sick with our sicknesses, to put our diseases away, and to bring us back to the Father. He did not die for Himself, but for us. He did not suffer for Himself, but for us. He was resurrected for us, His Body.

**The Body of Christ functions corporately to uphold the standards of the Kingdom of God. The Body is authorized by the name of Jesus and operates through spiritual laws to act as a single entity. It is composed of millions of members who are legally endowed with rights and duties.**

Our Father God wants to restore spiritual sight and understanding to the Body by giving us a clear revelation that we are *one Body* and that we are to lose our individual identities for the sake of the whole Body.

The Lord's Table, or the Communion, is a revelation of our oneness. As we partake of the bread, representing Christ's broken body, and the cup, representing His shed blood, we become one with Him and one with each other. As we eat His flesh, we become one flesh. As we drink of His blood, we become one blood. In a physical sense, nutritionists tell us, we become what we eat. So it is that we also become what we consume in a spiritual sense.

Communion is not just a rite, but an affirmation of the indissoluble blood covenant we have with Christ. It is a covenant of love that produces life. The moment a covenant is solemnized between two people, everything that each person owns is at the disposal of the other if he needs it. Love is the cord that binds us together.

Amazingly, this Body that is bound together by love is composed of millions of believers, and its members are increasing continually. It is placed in the midst of a world of darkness to become a glorious light that will fill the earth as man is reconciled to God. This Body reaches into every continent, nation, and people group and to the farthest corners of the earth. This giant Body is so large that it reaches from earth to Heaven, where the Head, who is Christ Himself, resides.

The Body lays claim to no particular color, tongue, or nationality. It is one Body, and there is to be no schism or division in the Body. There is to be no dissension or conflict. There is one Body and one Spirit. The Body's life is that which is lived in Christ.

The parts of the Body are interconnected. It can be said that each member has power, but like an automobile, that member can go much faster and farther if he is willing to lose his identity and become a part of the whole. The members of the Body must work as a team, each member working for the good of the entire Body. Teamwork requires that each member lay aside his or her own desires and do only those things that benefit the team. There must be a yielding of each member to the others and to the Holy Spirit, who is in the midst of the Body. The Holy Spirit helps us overcome our infirmities. He lives within us, joining with us, so that He might strengthen us where we are weak.

The ministry of the Holy Spirit works in the life of each believer. He is not limited to being in one place at a time as Jesus was when He was on earth. He indwells the entire Body and serves as the very breath that gives life to the Body.

The government of this Body is under the authority of the Lord Jesus Christ. Collectively, we are His Body. We are not an organization, religion, or denomination. We are an organism.

> *There is one body, and one Spirit, even as ye are called in one hope of your calling; one Lord, one faith, one baptism, one God and Father of all, who is above all, and through all, and in you all. But unto every one of us is given grace according to the measure of the gift of Christ. Wherefore he saith, When he ascended up on high, he led captivity captive, and gave gifts unto men. (Now that he ascended, what is it but that he also descended first into the lower parts of the earth? He that*

*descended is the same also that ascended up far above all heavens, that he might fill all things.) And he gave some, apostles; and some, prophets; and some, evangelists; and some, pastors and teachers; for the perfecting of the saints, for the work of the ministry, for the edifying of the body of Christ: till we all come in the unity of the faith, and of the knowledge of the Son of God, unto a perfect man, unto the measure of the stature of the fullness of Christ.* Ephesians 4:4-13

This passage of Scripture describes the coming together in unity of the Body. Currently in the natural and the spiritual realms a parallel is occurring in corporate bodies. In the natural realm, we see large corporations, banks, and media merging together. *Merge* means, "to cause to combine, unite, or coalesce," and "to blend gradually by stages that blur distinctions." Similarly, in the spiritual world we are witnessing the merging together of the Body of Christ. Retreats, conferences, and other types of spiritual meetings are attracting believers from all denominations. These hungry believers are seeking a fresh touch from God and are willingly uniting for worship, prayer, and fellowship at these gatherings.

*Behold, how good and how pleasant it is for brethren to dwell together in unity!* Psalm 133:1

My prayer is that this book will speak to the members of the Body of Christ, causing "Body consciousness" that will lead to the coming together and blending of the many streams of ministry. As the individual members come together, we will begin to flow as one mighty army, connecting with one another to produce wholeness in the Body of Christ.

Whatever our placement may be in the Body, whether we are the eyes, mouth, heart, legs, or some other part, we must function as we have been anointed to function, even as the human body functions with all its organs, systems, senses, and bones. Not every member or ministry has the same assignment or mission. Each of us has a work to perform to bring about the wholeness of the Body.

May the spirit of revelation and knowledge come upon you as you read this study of the Body.

*And wisdom and knowledge shall be the stability of thy times, and strength of salvation.* Isaiah 33:6

# 1 - Can These Bones Live?

*And he said unto me, Son of man, can these bones live? And I answered, O Lord GOD, thou knowest. Again he said unto me, Prophesy upon these bones, and say unto them, O ye dry bones, hear the word of the LORD. Thus saith the Lord GOD unto these bones; Behold, I will cause breath to enter into you, and ye shall live: and I will lay sinews upon you, and will bring up flesh upon you, and cover you with skin, and put breath in you, and ye shall live; and ye shall know that I am the LORD. So I prophesied as I was commanded: and as I prophesied, there was a noise, and behold a shaking, and the bones came together, bone to his bone. And when I beheld, lo, the sinews and the flesh came up upon them, and the skin covered them above: but there was no breath in them. Then said he unto me, Prophesy unto the wind, prophesy, son of man, and say to the wind, Thus saith the Lord GOD; Come from the four winds, O breath, and breathe upon these slain,*

*that they may live. So I prophesied as he commanded me, and the breath came into them, and they lived, and stood up upon their feet, an exceeding great army.*
Ezekiel 37:3-10

In the Old Testament, the prophet Ezekiel received this prophetic word for the House of Judah. God was telling Ezekiel that He was going to restore His people once again. Often events in the Old Testament foreshadowed events to come during the New Testament age. While this word of restoration was spoken for the nation of Israel, it can also apply to the Body of Christ.

Sin had caused man's image to become distorted, and he became disjoined from God. Man was no longer able to relate with God as God had intended. He was now separated from God and had taken on a new image—the image of the beast, or Satan. Jesus Christ came to bring reconciliation between man and God. He gave His life to give us life. Because of His sacrifice, He paved the way back, so that man could be made whole again, restored to the likeness and image of God. Also, Jesus gives man the power to overcome sin and become "*a living sacrifice, holy, acceptable unto God*" (Romans 12:1).

The valley of dry bones speaks of Israel's restoration, but it also speaks of God's plan to raise up a corporate body of believers—the Body of Christ.

When the hand of the Lord came upon Ezekiel and carried him away in the Spirit, he saw the vision of the dry bones. Ezekiel observed that these bones were "*very dry*" (Ezekiel 37:2). This observation raises the question,

How did the bones get so dry in the first place? We can find the answer in Proverbs 17:22.

*A broken spirit drieth the bones.*

## Dry Bones

Man was deceived by Satan and in his fallen state became the living dead. Satan separated him from God, causing that relationship to be broken. Man was no longer a god-man, but received a new name and image because he was now ruled by a new master, and in the process of his reeducation, he was thrust into an unfamiliar world. Without his relationship with God, he no longer reflected the glory of God. Because man did not have the image of God, he no longer had vision, because God provides vision. Man was now unable to see himself—his light had gone out. He was now in a state of deadness and dryness; he was disjointed, dismembered, and separated from his Creator.

Ezekiel's prophecy to the dry bones was a picture, or a foreshadowing, of God's intentions for man. God had Ezekiel prophesy to the dry bones so that they could be put back together again in the proper order. In order to remake the bones into living beings, Ezekiel would have to start with the original materials, and God would breathe life into them.

Just as He did with the bones that Ezekiel saw, God would once again breathe life into another set of "dry bones"—the Body of Christ. This time He would not breathe life into mere men, but into a super man with a supernatural body in which the Holy Spirit resided.

From the time of Christ and down through the generations, dryness invaded the Body of Christ in the form of the spirit of division, causing the Body to separate on issues such as doctrine, denominations, independence, individuality, and race.

The dry-bones condition of the Body speaks of coldness, weakness, indifference, complacency, and lack of love. A body without breath or spirit is a dead body. Adam's body was simply a lump of clay until God breathed life into his nostrils. Ezekiel's prophesying to dry bones shows us God's intent to restore life into the Body of Christ.

In the book of Ezekiel, God said that He would lay sinews upon the bones. What is a *sinew*? Webster's dictionary defines a *sinew* as "a chief supporting force," or "a cord or thread with resilient strength." Resilient strength gives one the ability to adjust to strain. A sinew can also be defined as a tendon, which is a tough cord of connective tissue that unites other parts and transmits the force that the muscle exerts.

Sinews connect the physical body together. They provide muscular power and vigorous strength. In order for the Body of Christ to be properly connected, member to member, ministry to ministry, denomination to denomination, it also must have supernatural power and strength.

When God told Ezekiel that He was going to lay sinew upon the bones, He was saying, "I am going to place supernatural power in My Body in this end time." And in Psalm 110:3, God said:

*Thy people shall be willing in the day of thy power.*

One interesting thing about the sinew is that the children of Israel were reluctant to eat this part of the animal.

> *Therefore the children of Israel eat not of the sinew which shrank, which is upon the hollow of the thigh, unto this day: because he touched the hollow of Jacob's thigh in the sinew that shrank.* Genesis 32:32

In further examining the word *sinew*, I divided it into syllables. The Greek word for *sin*, the first syllable, is *hamartia*, which means, "missing the mark."

Romans 6:6 tells us that sin has a body. From this verse of Scripture, we see that sinew is organized power acting through the members of the body. The syllable *ew* comes from the Greek word *epecho* which means, "to hold upon." If we put the two together, it would mean "holding upon in order not to miss the mark."

The Greek word for *hold* is *teresis*, which means, "a keeping, as commandments."

Not only did God lay sinews upon the bones, but He said He would bring flesh upon them as well. In this day, the Holy Spirit is working to bring about God-like character. This is a time when we will not see the power of God operating in the lives of unholy men and women. The nature and character of God will be the flesh of the Body of Christ.

In this human body, the skin covering the bones and sinews is important to the physical well-being of the body—the skin serves as protection. In the Body of Christ, the skin correlates with the covering of protection that God provides.

Job said,

> *Thou hast clothed me with skin and flesh, and hast fenced me with bones and sinews.*     Job 10:11

*Fence* means, "a protection or a barrier intended to prevent escape or intrusion." The skin of the flesh correlates with the covering that God provides for the Body of Christ. God covers His people with His love, protection, and authority. The skin of His covering serves as a barrier, or a protection.

Ezekiel was lastly instructed to call upon the wind to breathe life into the restored flesh before him. In Scripture, breath or wind refers to the presence of the Spirit. Today, the winds of the Spirit are blowing upon the Body of Christ and reviving the dry bones. The winds of the Spirit will pave the way for the end-time anointing that brings new life to the Body.

The Holy Spirit breathes life into the Body of Christ. Having the muscle without life in the Body is useless. Bones, sinews, flesh, and breath are all required.

The winds of the Spirit also serve to purge and purify the Body. In recent years, the winds have come to try every member and every ministry. Those who have allowed God to purge have become anchored in Christ and have been prepared for the storms to come. Those who have not allowed God to blow upon them and have run away from the tests, the afflictions, and have taken another route will not be able to stand in this day. Their faith will falter. They have not allowed themselves to receive the strength necessary to stand in this day. The winds of adversity and prosperity have come not only to try our roof in the rain, but also to try our very foundations. Those foundations built upon the Rock, Christ Jesus, will be able to stand.

In Ezekiel, the work of the wind is the final part of the restoration of the dry bones. The wind finishes restoration to the original state. In other words, God is saying through Ezekiel, "I am going to raise up a supernatural people who know what it means to be connected and united with cords of love that cannot be broken. Ministries will join together; believers will join together, creating a giant network that crosses all boundaries of race, culture, and geography."

The prophet Joel describes this mighty army of believers that will come together to form the Body in the last days.

> *They shall run like mighty men; they shall climb the wall like men of war; and they shall march every one on his ways, and they shall not break their ranks: neither shall one thrust another; they shall walk every one in his path: and when they fall upon the sword, they shall not be wounded. They shall run to and fro in the city; they shall run upon the wall, they shall climb up*

*upon the houses; they shall enter in at the windows like a thief. The earth shall quake before them; the heavens shall tremble: the sun and the moon shall be dark, and the stars shall withdraw their shining: and the LORD shall utter his voice before his army: for his camp is very great: for he is strong that executeth his word: for the day of the LORD is great and very terrible; and who can abide it?* Joel 2:7-11

## The Shaking

A second work of the Holy Spirit in these last days, besides the restoring to life of the Body, is a shaking loose of things that have been bound. There is a noise and a shaking among the women in the Body of Christ—they are being shaken loose from centuries of bondage. In order for the Body to freely function as it was designed, no member or members can be bound in any way. Every part must function as it was originally intended.

*To shake* means, "to cause to move to and fro," or "to bring to a specified condition by or as if by repeated quick jerky movements to free oneself, or by a pronounced movement."

Jeremiah 31:22 reads:

*How long wilt thou go about, O thou backsliding daughter? for the LORD hath created a new thing in the earth, A woman shall compass a man.*

The Greek word *kainos* means, "new," as in "that which

is unaccustomed or unused. Not new in time, but new as to form or quality." Prior to Jesus' ministry, women had little role in the formal traditions of the Jewish faith. Things changed with the coming of the Christ.

In Luke 24, we see an example of the significance of the role of women in the life and death of Jesus. Mary Magdalene, Joanna, and Mary, Jesus' mother, went to the sepulcher bringing spices to anoint the body of Jesus. When they arrived, they found the stone had been rolled away, and discovered the body of the Lord Jesus to be missing. Instead of Him, they saw two men in shining garments—angels—who told them that He was not there but had risen. The women left the sepulcher and went and told the disciples all that they had seen. Here we see that it was the women who had come to *"compass a man,"* the man being Jesus. No men had come to the tomb, just the women. In fact, the men didn't come until the women ran to tell them what had happened. At first the men didn't even believe them.

> *And their words seemed to them as idle tales, and they believed them not.*           Luke 24:11

It was Peter who finally went to see for himself. Followed by John, he went to the sepulcher and found it empty. In spite of all the times the Lord had explained to His disciples that He would first die and then rise on the third day, none of the men had gone to the tomb. It took the faith of the women to lead the men to the truth. Was this event a foreshadowing of the end-time role of women? Will women bring an anointing to the Body of Christ?

In this day, we see God doing a work in the lives of women. There is a great shaking, and women are beginning to receive such a great anointing that men will be astonished at what God is doing in and through women.

For many centuries in the Church, women have been bound and not able to operate in ministry as men have. Women have been told that they have not been called to the ministry. But if we go back to the scripture in Jeremiah 31:22, we find a different message. What does this verse mean when it says, *"A woman shall compass a man"*?

The Greek word for *compass* (or encompass) is *kukloo*, which means, "to move in a circle." *Compass* also means, "to get into one's possession or power." Women will have a major role in the awakening that is taking place in the body of Christ at this time.

As women are being loosed to minister in this day, they will bring alignment to the body of Christ. A woman will compass a man in the sense that women have a key role to play in this day. There is neither male nor female in the role of ministry.

Ephesians 4:11 says, *"He gave some."* The word *some* refers to those who received gifts of office, and it does not specify male or female.

> *And he gave some, apostles; and some, prophets; and some evangelists; and some, pastors and teachers.*
> Ephesians 4:11

This is going to shake the theology of some, and they may find it a bitter pill to swallow, but there must be a liberating of the whole Body of Christ before it becomes that Bride adorned to meet Christ. Such a great anointing is going to come upon women that men will rethink their position that it takes a man to get the job done. In one respect the male perspective is true—the Man, Christ Jesus, is getting the job done. But when it comes to the Body of Christ, the whole Body must function at full capacity or it is weakened.

Looking back into the Garden of Eden, we need to ask, "Why did the serpent approach the woman?" The serpent approached the woman because she had the womb, the doorway of life. Through the woman, the seed of disobedience would enter into the physical realm. To birth anything into the physical world, there has to be intimate contact.

The same is true of a rebirth of the Spirit into the Body of Christ. Before the coming of the Lord, the Body will enter into a time of great revival and awakening, the Body's intimate contact with the Spirit. The awakening, the new life in the Body, will come through the womb of the Bride, through intimate contact with the Spirit.

When Ezekiel was told to prophesy to the dry bones and tell them to live, he was speaking to everyone in the Body, not to just a few. Woman began as a rib, and the Hebrew word for *rib* means, "of the body." Therefore, every part of the Body of Christ will be restored to its proper function, including women.

The question we must ask for today is, Can these millions of people, members of the Body of Christ, live? Can there be a coming together of the bones of the Body of Christ? Can every joint fulfill its part? Can every single believer fulfill his or her purpose? Can each member give to the Body the portion that has been given to him or her?

A bone must be fitly joined in the proper place in order to receive the proper nourishment for life. When a bone becomes separated from the source of life, it becomes dry. There is life and wholeness in being properly fitted into the Body. This means the Body must experience unity for its own proper function and good health.

God said that He would lay sinews upon the Body. In order for the parts of the Body to make the proper connections, the Body must have the necessary strength and power. The prophet Joel prophesied that in the last days God would pour out His Spirit on all flesh. The Body of Christ, though a spiritual entity, is comprised of flesh. We can therefore say that the Body of Christ will be supernaturally anointed for the end time.

Ezekiel was told to prophesy words of life to the bones:

*Thus saith the Lord GOD unto these bones; Behold, I will cause breath to enter into you, and ye shall live* [or have life]. Ezekiel 37:5

# 2 - Jesus Christ: The Seed of the Woman

At the birth of a child, the first thing to emerge from the womb is the head. The same is also true for the Body of Christ. The Head, Jesus, would be birthed first. The promise of this birth was first spoken of in the book of Genesis.

Sin had separated Adam and Eve from God, who is the fountain of life. They had been exposed to Satan (the serpent), who was spiritually infected and already defiled. The effects of their sin spread to all of mankind. Eve, the woman, was the door through which sin gained entrance into the earth. Sorrow filled Adam's and Eve's hearts, and in mercy God promised them He would send One who would come to destroy the works of Satan and redeem man from sin.

> *And I will put enmity between thee and the woman, and between thy seed and her seed; it shall bruise thy head, and thou shalt bruise his heel.* Genesis 3:15

Forty-two generations passed, and then it was time for that prophetic word to be fulfilled. In order to introduce the undefiled seed that would redeem man, God prepared a new body. This body would be physically born into the world while bearing a pure spiritual Seed from Heaven. The apostle Paul described the coming of Jesus this way:

> *Wherefore when he cometh into the world, he saith, Sacrifice and offering thou wouldest not, but a body hast thou prepared me.*           Hebrews 10:5

To redeem man, God would need to be born as a man. This required birth through a woman. God chose a virgin through whom the Seed of the woman would come. The prophetic word of the Lord came to Mary through an angel who visited her and said:

> *Hail, thou that art highly favoured, the Lord is with thee: blessed art thou among women.... Fear not, Mary: for thou hast found favour with God. And, behold, thou shalt conceive in thy womb, and bring forth a son, and shalt call his name JESUS. He shall be great, and shall be called the Son of the Highest: and the Lord God shall give unto him the throne of his father David: and he shall reign over the house of Jacob for ever; and of his kingdom there shall be no end.*
>           Luke 1:28, 30-33

Jesus came through the genealogy of Joseph. He came to earth by way of the birth process. He was conceived in the womb of a virgin by the Holy Spirit through the overshadowing of the Highest.

Jesus came to earth not as one adorned in royal robes and living in the splendor of a palace like an earthly king, but He was born in a stable with a manger for His cradle. He came to become the Lamb of God, the undefiled One.

Jesus' coming represented a new covenant. Before the coming forth of the new, the old must die. The ax had to be laid to the root of the tree. This meant that God would create a severing from the old covenant in order to make room for the new one. God would assign someone to begin this process.

Six months before Jesus' conception, Mary's cousin Elizabeth conceived a son in her old age. Elizabeth's son, John the Baptist, was born to be the forerunner of Jesus. His mission was to prepare the way for the coming of the promised Seed, Jesus. It was John who began preaching the baptism of repentance in preparation for the coming ministry of the Messiah.

John was born to a barren woman who was also beyond the childbearing age. When God is about to do something that will change the lives of men, He often uses barrenness. In this, no man will be able to take credit—creating life from nothing is a supernatural happening, which can only be accomplished by God. Elizabeth's womb was barren, and could not physically bear a child; her womb was preserved, shut up in the natural, not shut out of God's purposes. At the appointed time, God opened her womb to fulfill His purpose—the birth of the forerunner of the Messiah.

John's birth was foretold to his parents this way: an angel appeared to the priest Zacharias as he performed his priestly duties in the Temple. The angel told Zacharias that his prayer had been heard and his wife, Elizabeth, would bear him a son and he should call his name John, and that many would rejoice at his birth. This son would be great in the sight of the Lord, would live the life of a Nazirite, would drink neither wine nor strong drink, and would be filled with the Holy Spirit from his mother's womb. The angel said, *"He shall go before him* [meaning, the Messiah] *in the spirit and power of Elias, to turn the hearts of the fathers to the children, and the disobedient to the wisdom of the just; to make ready a people prepared for the Lord"* (Luke 1:17).

John prepared the way for Jesus. When he emerged into ministry, he began to preach the baptism of repentance for the remission of sins. He proclaimed the approach of the Kingdom of Heaven. This Kingdom would be the realm in which the will of God would be fulfilled.

In the first covenant, the commandments had been given to the Israelites in the wilderness, but man could not keep the Law. Jesus came not to do away with the Law, but to fulfill the Law.

John's birth, life, and ministry created the expectation that a great one was about to appear, and this brought a great multitude out to see him.

John was a prophet, and much about his life was a prophetic demonstration of the state of man. He lived by himself in the wilderness, representing man's separation from God. The timing of his birth was six months before

*Jesus Christ: The Seed of the Woman*

the birth of Jesus, a prophetic sign of the One who was coming to redeem man. The number six represents man biblically because man was created on the sixth day.

John's garment was camel's hair and was attached to his body by a leather girdle. The bristle of this garment was a constant reminder of the curse on man: a life of thorns and thistles and the reluctance of the earth to give its increase. His food was locusts and wild honey, the food of the wilderness.

John baptized his disciples. The baptism, or immersion in water, was a symbol of the cleansing of man's life. It represented a cleaning of the slate of previous wrongdoing in preparation for the coming of the Kingdom of Heaven. John did not preach about himself. His life demonstrated self-denial, humility, and courage. He declared that he was merely a voice calling for people to prepare for the reception of the One whose shoe latches he was not worthy to unloose. About the One who was to come, John said, *"He must increase, but I must decrease"* (John 3:30).

Jesus, the Seed of the woman, was born in a stable in Bethlehem. The angels announced His birth.

> *And there were in the same country shepherds abiding in the field, keeping watch over their flock by night. And, lo, the angel of the Lord came upon them, and the glory of the Lord shone round about them: and they were sore afraid. And the angel said unto them, Fear not: for, behold, I bring you good tidings of great joy, which shall be to all people. For unto you is born*

> *this day in the city of David a Saviour, which is Christ the Lord. And this shall be a sign unto you; Ye shall find the babe wrapped in swaddling clothes, lying in a manger."* Luke 2:8-12

What a befitting place it was for the Lamb of God to be born. How appropriate it was for the announcement to be given to shepherds. There was no room in the inn for Him to be born—an inn was not a proper place for the birth of a lamb.

Jesus came to bring a new order, the righteous rule of God on earth. The name *Jesus* means, "Savior," and the word *Christ* means, "anointed one." He came anointed as Savior to redeem mankind, to restore God's family to Himself.

> *For as by one man's disobedience many were made sinners, so by the obedience of one shall many be made righteous.* Romans 5:19

The prophet Isaiah, who lived several hundred years before Jesus was born, spoke additional prophetic words concerning the coming of the Savior.

> *Arise, shine; for thy light is come, and the glory of the LORD is risen upon thee. For, behold, the darkness shall cover the earth, and gross darkness the people: but the LORD shall arise upon thee, and his glory shall be seen upon thee. And the Gentiles shall come to thy light, and kings to the brightness of thy rising.*
> Isaiah 60:1-3

Though Christ came to reconcile man back to God, He was not recognized by men as the promised Seed of the woman.

*He was in the world, and the world was made by him, and the world knew him not. He came unto his own, and his own received him not. But as many as received him, to them gave he power to become the sons of God, even to them that believe on his name: which were born, not of blood, nor of the will of the flesh, nor of the will of man, but of God.* John 1:10-13

Jesus came, suffered, and died that we might have life and have it more abundantly. He was hung up for all our hang-ups. He hung on a tree and died. It was a curse to be hung on a tree. The Bible speaks of men as being like trees.

*...that they might be called trees of righteousness, the planting of the LORD, that he might be glorified.*
Isaiah 61:3

If man is a tree, why should He hang on a tree? This speaks of man being separated from his roots, the part of the tree from which he receives his food for life.

God first created man in His likeness and image and placed him in a perfect environment where he could freely partake of the trees in the Garden of Eden. He had the freedom to eat from the tree of life, but was to abstain from eating from the tree of the knowledge of good and evil. Man disobeyed and was expelled from the Garden.

But God did not give up in His desire to have to fellowship with man. He still desired to commune with man and to have man oversee His creation in the earthly realm.

After man, namely Adam and Eve, fell into disobedience, God sought another man who would obey Him and walk with Him in holiness and righteousness. He found this man in Abraham, who was willing to give up everything in obedience to God.

Abraham became the center of God's plan for restoration. God told Abraham that because of him, all the families of the earth would be blessed. God chose a people from the seed of Abraham, and from that people came the Seed of the woman, who would form a new Body, the Body of Christ.

The night Jesus was arrested we see the beginning of the birthing of the Body of Christ. The pains of labor began. In physical labor, the head of the child is in the birth canal. The head comes forth first. In a spiritual sense, Jesus is the Head of the Body of Christ. He is the firstborn from the dead. In physical birth, as the baby moves down the birth canal, great pressure is felt, and a bloody show appears. In relating this to the spiritual birth of the Body, Isaiah tells us,

> *But he was wounded for our transgressions, he was bruised for our iniquities: the chastisement of our peace was upon him; and with his stripes we are healed.... He was oppressed, and he was afflicted, yet he opened not his mouth: he is brought as a lamb to the slaughter, and as a sheep before her shearers is dumb, so he openeth not his mouth.*     Isaiah 53:5,7

From the physical perspective, contractions begin, the amniotic sac breaks, and active labor begins. During the birthing of the Body, contractions began at Jesus' arrest. He was beaten and mocked by the temple guards. When He was turned over to the Romans, He received thirty-nine stripes with the whip, and then He was scourged. His flesh was literally ripped open and His blood flowed out of the wounds and onto the ground. He was then condemned to die by crucifixion, the cruelest type of execution performed by the Roman military.

Before He was crucified, He suffered great indignities at the hands of the Roman soldiers. They stripped Him, and put a scarlet robe on Him, an imitation of what kings wore. Then they forced a plaitted crown of thorns onto His head. A reed was pressed into His hand as a mock scepter, and they spit on Him. They took the reed and smote Him on the head. After they had mocked Him and abused Him as much as they wanted to, they led Him away to be crucified at a place called Golgotha, which means, "place of a skull." This was a place where the bones and skulls of dead men were laid.

Jesus' hands and feet were nailed to a wooden cross that was set upright and dropped down into a hole just deep enough to keep the cross standing. When they nailed Him to the cross, the soldiers stripped Him of His garments and then they divided His garments among themselves and cast lots for His inner garment. On a board they nailed above His head, they wrote the accusation against Him:

*THIS IS JESUS THE KING OF THE JEWS.*
                                                    Matthew 27:37

The usual drink given to those being crucified was a cup of wine, but to Jesus they offered a drink containing vinegar mingled with gall, to make it sour and bitter. He tasted it but would not drink it.

Death by crucifixion was a slow death of suffocation. Jesus pulled or pushed upward against the nails in order to breathe. This struggle would last for hours.

From the sixth hour there was darkness over all the land until the ninth hour.

> *And about the ninth hour Jesus cried with a loud voice, saying, Eli, Eli, lama sabachthani? that is to say, My God, my God, why hast thou forsaken me?*
> Matthew 27:46

> *Jesus, when he had cried again with a loud voice, yielded up the ghost. And, behold, the veil of the temple was rent in twain from the top to the bottom; and the earth did quake, and the rocks rent; and the graves were opened; and many bodies of the saints which slept arose.* Matthew 27:50-52

After His death, Jesus' body was taken down from the cross and placed in a nearby grave. The labor pains had climaxed, but the best was yet to come.

For those who are participating in the birth of a child, the most exciting part is when the baby's head crowns, or appears, to where it can be seen. Three days after Jesus' death, He emerged from that grave, resurrected from the dead. The Head of the Body had emerged! With the resurrection of Christ, the rest of the Body would follow Him into life in the days that followed.

## 3 – Ye Are the Body

*But now is Christ risen from the dead, and become the firstfruits of them that slept. For since by man came death, by man came also the resurrection of the dead. For as in Adam all die, even so in Christ shall all be made alive.*     1 Corinthians 15:20-22

The birth of the Body of Christ would follow the birthing of the Head. Christ is called the last Adam: the seed of obedience. The Church is His Body—the entire matter, structure, and substance of Him. The Body of Christ, the Church, was born out of His side, even as the woman was taken out of Adam's body. *"Ye are the body"* (1 Corinthians 12:27).

*For by one Spirit are we all baptized into one body, whether we be Jews or Gentiles, whether we be bond or free; and have been all made to drink into one Spirit.*
    1 Corinthians 12:13

Because of the fall of the first Adam, death began to reign on earth. It was necessary for Jesus to take the sting out of death and get the victory over the grave. The Seed had to fall into the ground and die. The seed of mankind had become corrupt and was, therefore, a seed of disobedience. Seeds reproduce after their kind. There had to be a replanting of the seed of obedience, a resurrection of the seed of life. The seed of the man in its fallen state had the ability to reproduce after its kind. The Seed of the woman had to be planted in the earth to restore man to his original state, or to cause a resurgence, or a raising again to life.

> *There is a natural body, and there is a spiritual body. And so it is written, The first man Adam was made a living soul; the last Adam was made a quickening spirit. Howbeit that was not first which is spiritual, but that which is natural; and afterward that which is spiritual. The first man is of the earth, earthy: the second man is the Lord from heaven. As is the earthy, such are they also that are earthy: and as is the heavenly, such are they also that are heavenly.*
> 1 Corinthians 15:44-48

The spiritual Body of Christ on earth, of which Christ is the Head, is composed of millions of members, each with a specific function to perform. This gigantic Body spreads from sea to sea, race to race, and nation to nation. Each member is placed in a specific part of the Body.

God has designed the Body as it pleased Him. It is of

heavenly origin. Our roots are found in Him. They go deeper than our earthly ethnic heritage.

Jesus said:

*I am the true vine, and my Father is the husbandman.*
John 15:1

It is interesting to note that Jesus likens Himself to a vine. A vine has a specialized ability for climbing and crawling along the ground and spreading, which speaks of the worldwide spreading of the Body of Christ on earth. Jesus also speaks of God the Father as being like the *"husbandman,"* or the planter of the vine. It is the planter who determines what type of vine to plant and where to plant it. He is also responsible for its care. This relates to the Father's role in relation to the Body.

God's goal is to restore man to His likeness and image. Jesus is the Head of that new man.

*Sacrifice and offering thou wouldest not, but a body hast thou prepared me.* Hebrews 10:5

Jesus willingly submitted to being scourged. He willingly allowed His back to be ripped open, and the lifeblood that was in His body spurted out and was absorbed into the earth that had been cursed because of sin. The lifeblood of God diffused into the earth.

*But he was wounded for our transgressions, he was*

> *bruised for our iniquities: the chastisement of our peace was upon him; and with his stripes we are healed.*
> Isaiah 53:5

Jesus' physical body was beaten, bruised, and bloodied so that the life of God could flow out from Him to you and me. His physical death gave life to the spiritual Body.

> *Yet it pleased the LORD to bruise him; he hath put him to grief: when thou shalt make his soul an offering for sin, he shall see his seed, he shall prolong his days, and the pleasure of the LORD shall prosper in His hand.*
> Isaiah 53:10

## 4 – Oneness in Christ

For any body to function properly, all the parts must work as a team, each doing its part, at the direction of the brain, or the head. Each part, whether it be a limb or an organ or some other part, must function in its design in relation to all the other parts around it, and at the direction of the head.

The same is true of the Body of Christ. God designed the Body to work as a unified organism. For the Body to function properly, all the members must function in their design, must coexist in relation to all the other parts, and must operate at the direction of the Head. This speaks of the Body being perfected.

*Perfecting* is from the Greek word *katartismos*, meaning "a fitting or preparing fully." When referring to the parts of the Body, this word describes a knitting together so that each part connects with the others to form a complete body.

*There is one body, and one Spirit, even as ye are called in one hope of your calling; one Lord, one faith, one baptism, one God and Father of all, who is above all, and through all, and in you all.* Ephesians 4:4-6

The Body of Christ is ideally joined together. Sin separated man from God, but Christ broke down the middle wall of partition and made it possible for man to once again have a right relationship with God.

*Behold, how good and how pleasant it is for brethren to dwell together in unity!* Psalm 133:1

Once restored to a right relationship with God, the new man, the Body of Christ, can once again worship God in the beauty of holiness as a unified organism. Worship is one of the power lines that connect all the members of the Body together. As we learn to worship God, we learn to relate to one another in our commonality. Individually we exist to praise and worship Him, but we also exist for those same reasons as members of the whole. God's divine intention was that man would have fellowship with Him and with each other.

*By this shall all men know that ye are my disciples, if ye have love one to another.* John 13:35

A second connection all the members share is the blood of Christ. The members of the Body are related to one another through the blood of Jesus. In a human body, blood is what carries life to each part of the body. It is

*Oneness in Christ*

what each part has in common with the rest. In the Body of Christ, Jesus' blood flowing through all of us gives us life.

The power and wonder of the blood is that it is not limited to one member or to one part of the Body. It is able to reach every member with its properties of healing, nourishing, and cleansing. There is a unifying power of the blood. We are of one blood whether we are of the black, white, yellow, or red race. There is no difference in blood. It is His blood that covers us all and sets us free from sin.

*And* [God] *hath made of one blood all nations of men for to dwell on all the face of the earth.* Acts 17:26

As the Body, we must also be concerned with the health of the whole organism. We must walk in love, peace, and joy, which are elements of good spiritual health. If we walk in envy, bitterness, and jealousy, we release toxins into the Body and endanger the health of it. If we attack one another verbally or physically, evil is released within the Body. When we go to one another's aid and act in love, we release antibodies that fight the toxins.

Our example must always be the Head, Jesus. Christ came in obedience to the Father. While He was on earth, He did the works of God. He didn't speak evil of His accusers or of those who crucified Him. He submitted to the will of His Father. There is power in a righteous response to evil that crushes the serpent's head. It tears evil out by the roots, out of our own hearts and out of the hearts of those who persecute us. Righteousness is our inoculation against spiritual diseases that could cripple or kill the Body, and Christ is our source for righteousness. He broke the power of sin and sickness to rescue us from an eternity of separation from God. He made the way for us to have a relationship with God the Father.

Sin marred the image of God in man who was made in the likeness of God, but that image has been given back through the new man, Christ. The Body of Christ reflects Him.

The Body of Christ is being transformed to reflect the glory of God. The Spirit of God is in the Body, and He undertakes to transform our nature and our character so that we may become like Him and reflect Him in all respects.

## 5 - Communion

Communion is God's promise of His presence. It is coming into oneness with Him and with the rest of the members of the Body. The word *communion* means, "friendship and fellowship." Fellowship says, "We are in this together. I cannot do without you, and you cannot do without me. My destiny is locked inside of you, and yours is locked inside of me. We need each other so that we both will be released into the fullness of our purpose."

### Eat My Flesh, Drink My Blood

Because Jesus' body was broken for us and His blood was shed for us, the Body can receive the promise of eternal communion with God the Father. Jesus said,

> *Whoso eateth my flesh, and drinketh my blood, hath eternal life; and I will raise him up at the last day.*
> John 6:54

Communion with God is represented by the ordinance of the Church known as Holy Communion. When we participate in Holy Communion, we are developing oneness with God because we are partaking of the flesh and blood of His Son, Jesus Christ. When we take of the bread and of the wine, we share in His likeness, His nature, and His character.

We all eat the same bread and drink the same wine and as we do, we identify with Christ. There is a blending together of Christ, as Head, and the Body. We become a part of each other. We become what we eat. This is one reason why the Israelites were commanded not to eat the blood of animals. The life of the flesh is in the blood. God did not want them to partake of the animal nature by eating the blood of animals. When we partake of Christ at the Communion table, we partake of His nature and thus become like Him.

> *Then Jesus said unto them, Verily, verily, I say unto you, Except ye eat the flesh of the Son of man, and drink his blood, ye have no life in you.*
>
> John 6:53

At the Communion table, everything that we need for life is present. The bread represents Jesus' flesh, which sustains us. The wine represents His blood, which saves us. The blood is also our lifeline. If we have received the lifeline, we can extend it to others to bring them to safety. That lifeline also gives us access to God through prayer so that we can present our petitions and requests to God and receive His answers.

## Let Us Break Bread Together

Though each member of the Body differs in his or her role and purpose, all the parts fitted together joint by joint create the whole. Communion calls the various parts back into the singularity of nature, character, and purpose of the Body as a whole. Our differences disappear. We are no longer race, but grace, and all of the parts receive access to God through the New Covenant, represented by the elements on the Communion table. The nature, character, and purpose of God then become visible to others outside of the Body through the fruit of the Spirit.

*Every good tree bringeth forth good fruit; but a corrupt tree bringeth forth evil fruit.* Matthew 7:17

Jesus, the Bread of Life, came to be broken for us, the Body. He did not come just to bless, but to be taken, to be broken, and to be given. When we break the Bread of Life together during Holy Communion, we create a oneness of spirit as well as a oneness of community.

The believers in the New Testament had an awareness of the importance of the breaking of bread during Communion, and they did not fail to honor the Communion as Christ had instructed. The Communion was not something they just did once in a while. They understood the significance of partaking of Christ's "body and blood" via the bread and wine, and they did so in remembrance of Him.

In the early Church that we read about in the book of Acts, the believers communed with one another by meeting in their homes.

*And they continued stedfastly in the apostles' doctrine and fellowship, and in breaking of bread, and in prayers.* Acts 2:42

During their gatherings it was customary for them to break bread together. Sharing a meal developed a closeness among them. They gained a oneness of community that gave them a sensitivity and a love for one another. The Scriptures say that these believers had all things common—each one shared what he or she had with those who did not have, and this was done so completely that there was no lack among them.

This is the way fellowship should be in the Body of Christ. If there is a lack in the Body, the Body is infirm. Infirmity in the Body will cause it to bend, or to bow, or to miss the purpose for which it was created.

Fellowship and sharing eliminate selfishness. The spirit of selfishness has destroyed families and nations, but sharing does the opposite—it draws us together. Just as sharing a meal with our family helps us to learn about our family members and draw closer to them, so also does sharing Holy Communion draw us together with other members of the Body. We begin to learn about each other. We become sensitive to one another's needs. We become helpers of one another. Sensitivity and compassion are developed, which would not be possible if we stayed separated from one another.

As members of the Body of Christ, we are like the different ingredients that go into the making of the bread. Each ingredient differs from the others, but when they are blended together, they become one with each other and they take on a new nature. They share fellowship in the bread.

We do not all come from the same race or background. Some of us had good parents, and some had bad parents.

But through Christ, we can blend and become one to feed the nations of the world. There can be a total blending that creates a new nature, one in which we love our neighbors as we love ourselves, and in which we develop complete dependence on each other, just like the ingredients in bread itself.

Can we perhaps receive revelation that will edify the Body from the ingredients in bread?

Flour comes from wheat.

> *Except a corn of wheat fall into the ground and die, it abideth alone: but if it die, it bringeth forth much fruit.*
> John 12:24

Because of Jesus' death and resurrection, many sons have come to God. And because of His example, we also learn to die to self.

Yeast is a leavening agent that causes bread to rise. It was necessary for Jesus to be raised from the dead.

> *And I, if I be lifted up from the earth, will draw all men unto me.*
> John 12:32

*Draw* means, "to cause to come near." Just as Jesus was raised to new life, we are also raised to new life through faith in Him.

Salt gives vitality and flavor. It also is a preserving agent.

> *Salt is good.... Have salt in yourselves, and have peace one with another."*
> Mark 9:50

Fats and liquids are for cohesiveness. Jesus said, *"I and my Father are one"* (John 10:30). Their relationship is cohesive just as Christ is cohesive with the Body. He promised His followers, *"I will never leave thee, nor forsake thee"* (Hebrews 13:5). The members of the Body should experience that same cohesion with one another.

Godly relationships *complete* each other, not *compete with* each other. If we cannot relate to one another, then we will never be able to relate to others outside of the Body, and thus we will never become effective ministers for Christ.

## 6 – Feeding the Multitudes

The main reason why Jesus left His Body on earth was so that the world could be evangelized. The work of the Body is to minister salvation and healing to the lost. Man was created with an innate spiritual hunger that needs to find nourishment in something, but because of sin, man is blind and cannot feed himself the truth of the Word of God. This mission is left up to the Body of Christ, to provide mankind with the proper spiritual nourishment he needs to live eternally. But in order for the Body to fulfill this role, each member must first be prepared for this work.

The feeding of the 5,000 is an illustration of how the Body is prepared for ministry. Within the illustration, we find the path that every believer must walk in order to be useful and fruitful in the Kingdom.

Before a believer can become a thriving, useful member of the Body, he or she must go through a process of sanctifying, cleansing, and renewing of the mind. It often has been said that affliction loosens sin from our soul.

In the story of the feeding of the 5,000, the multitude had followed Jesus and they were hungry. Jesus asked Philip where they were going to find enough food to feed the crowd. He asked Philip this as a test, because He already knew what He was going to do. Andrew, another one of the disciples, told Him that they had found a lad who had five barley loaves and two small fishes, but that this little bit of food was not enough to feed so many.

Jesus was preparing to do a miracle. Though they only had a little food, little in the hands of Jesus is much. He has the power of multiplication. Read the directions Jesus gave to His disciples.

> *And Jesus took the loaves; and when he had given thanks, he distributed to the disciples, and the disciples to them that were set down; and likewise of the fishes as much as they would. When they were filled, he said unto his disciples, Gather up the fragments that remain, that nothing be lost. Therefore they gathered them together, and filled twelve baskets with the fragments of the five barley loaves, which remained over and above unto them that had eaten.*
>
> John 6:11-13

We can learn the following principles about preparation for ministry in these elements of the story.

First, Jesus gave thanks to God. To mature as a member of the Body, we must first learn to live a life of thanksgiving to God, who is the Giver of life. Giving is the seed of receiving. It is the key element in God's character. We cannot expect to receive blessings without planting the seeds of thanksgiving. God gave everything He had for man and to man, and we thank Him to acknowledge that we recognize where our blessings come from and to keep ourselves from falling into the sin of pride.

Second, Jesus broke the bread and the fishes. He separated them into pieces. In order for the loaves to be given, they could not remain intact. Likewise, we as believers must be broken. We must learn that nothing we accomplish is done in our own strength. We are only useful to God after we have passed through the fires of failure and defeat of our natural abilities, and after we have realized that we can do nothing on our own, no matter how talented we may be. Our abilities must be sacrificed on the altar, to be given back to us by God so we are anointed with His power and approval. Once we are broken we will also realize that we are not the whole "loaf." We are only a portion and we need the other members of the Body to be complete. Each individual, each ministry, has something to impart to the rest of the Body.

Third, Jesus gave the food to the disciples to be given to the people. We have nothing to give to the world unless He gives it to us. We receive from Him by communing with Him, by praying, worshiping, and meditating in the Word of God. We need to be in His presence, see His face, and allow His face to be our reflection, our image. What we take in we become. Christ has to first feed us before we can feed others.

Fourth, the disciples gave the food to the multitude.

What we have received from Him in our time with Him becomes life to others. If we receive life, we can give life. Life begets life. Death begets death.

After the feeding of the 5,000, there were twelve baskets of food left. Twelve is the number of order and government. Jesus had twelve disciples. It is significant that twelve were left. Twelve represents a nucleus, or a center. The twelve disciples represented the nucleus of His Body. From those twelve would come all those who would believe in Him. These twelve would be assigned the important task of feeding the Body itself. We can read about Jesus' commissioning of them for this duty in the twenty-first chapter of John. Here, Jesus appeared to His disciples before He ascended to Heaven. He came to feed them in order to prepare them for their ministry to the Body.

Jesus said to Simon Peter,

*Simon, son of Jonas, lovest thou me more than these? He saith unto him, Yea, Lord; thou knowest that I love thee. He saith unto him, Feed my lambs. He saith to him again the second time, Simon, son of Jonas, lovest thou me? He saith unto him, Yea, Lord; thou knowest that I love thee. He saith unto him, Feed my sheep. He saith unto him the third time, Simon, son of Jonas, lovest thou me? Peter was grieved because he said unto him the third time, Lovest thou me? And he said unto him, Lord, thou knowest all things; thou knowest that I love thee. Jesus said unto him, Feed my sheep.*
John 21:15-17

Jesus said, "If you love Me, you will keep My commandments" (see John 14:15). Jesus fed the disciples to provide for them an example. He had fed them and in turn they were to feed his "sheep," who would make up the Body. In order to meet the needs of the world, the Body would first need to be fed so that it would grow strong.

Jesus told Peter the first time to feed His lambs. When new members are born into the Body of Christ, they must feed on the sincere milk of the Word. They must receive the same care that is given to newborn babies. They must be taught how to walk in their faith, how to talk in their faith, and how to discern the things of the Spirit.

It is interesting that Jesus emphasized the feeding of His sheep by commanding Peter twice to feed them. Many sheep will come into the local church bruised, wounded, and half dead, needing the shepherd to pour in the oil and the wine and to care for them until they are nursed back to health. Some will come in constipated, full of wrong doctrines that must be eliminated. This sometimes takes time and patience, and can only be done through love. But it is imperative that it be done. If the Body is not healthy, who will feed the rest of the world?

There would be other disciples who would follow these first twelve. Those who would come later would also have sufficient food to feed future generations. As one of those who have followed, are you willing to be broken and poured out for others? Jesus became bread for us. Will you become bread so that others might live?

*The cup of blessing which we bless, is it not the communion of the blood of Christ? The bread which we break, is it not the communion of the body of Christ? For we being many are one bread, and one body: for we are all partakers of that one bread.*
1 Corinthians 10:16-17

# 7 - The Body Is Not One Member

*For the body is not one member, but many. If the foot shall say, Because I am not the hand, I am not of the body; is it therefore not of the body?*
1 Corinthians 12:14-15

One day, this dialogue began to repeat itself over and over in my mind. As I focused on it and gave serious thought to it I saw that, it illustrates how sometimes members of the Body of Christ have the wrong focus.

What if the blood began to say, "Wow! I am really important because I transport oxygen and cell-building materials for the body. Without me the body would be nothing"?

What if the veins say to the blood, "You really think you are in the flow of things, right? Listen, I carry you. Without me, you would be spurting all over the body. I am your container; I give you form"?

These Bones Will Live

Now let's suppose that the heart hears the argument and joins in to say, "The two of you just be quiet. I'll solve this matter for you. I am the center of attention. Without me, there would be no circulatory system. There would be nothing to receive blood and pump it through the arteries. Have you not noticed that my location is in the center of the body? That should tell you something."

Then the lungs join in, saying, "Wait a minute, heart. You may have a central location, but if I don't supply you with oxygen, just see how long you will last!"

The stomach laughs, "Ha, ha, ha! If I shut down the digestive system, which stimulates the waste system, then see if we won't have a problem!"

Skin says to all of them, "I have listened to this argument and at first I thought to just ignore you all, but I began to think. Everyone might say that I am just flesh, but without me you would really be exposed."

The bones say, "That's right, and without my frame you would be void and without form. I cause you to connect, I cause you to relate, and I cause you to join, so that every joint can fulfill its part. I am your connector."

The eyes jump in and add, "Enough! That's enough of this silly argument. I am the window of the body—without me you all would be in darkness, not knowing where you are going."

At this the brain says to the eyes, "You think you guide the body, right? Not so! I am the control center. I receive sensations, and I give the interpretation. I control the muscles."

The legs say, "Yeah, brain, that's so. But if I fall off, can you cause the body to walk?"

The hands then rise up to speak. "I have listened to the points that each of you presented. Yes, I agree that we are all members of the body. Each one of us is important for the correct functioning of the body. Look at me as I am lifted in praise to God."

This kind of thinking actually exists within the Body among the believers. Some of us actually believe we are more important than the other members, that our contribution to the Body is more vital, or more necessary. To all of the members, I say, Beloved, let us examine our relationships one to another. We all need each other, but there is a higher authority. We are all under authority of our Head; Christ is the Head of our Body. And we are all necessary for the proper functioning of the Body. Yes, "brain," you have been given great responsibility, and yes, "heart," you are in the center, but you are not the center of the universe. We all must obey Christ's authority because our existence, our functions, and our activities depend on Him. Without Him, we can do nothing. We must function as we have been assigned.

Each member of the Body supplies a need of the Body and receives a supply from the Body. We must fellowship with, respect, and value one another. We are in this Body together. "Mouth," you can speak. "Ear," you can hear. "Blood," you can flow. Yet none of you can live by your own supply, but only from the life that comes from the Body.

In the Body there are no "free agents." Freedom and individuality are costly to the Body. Wild cells or malignant ones cause illness or even death. Every part must respond to the authority of the Head. We call our own shots in sections or as individuals. We must dwell together as one in unity and harmony under the headship of Christ.

There should be no schism in the Body. The natural body as well as the spiritual Body of Christ have been created and the members placed in them as God pleased. We simply have to become what we have been created to be in the Body. The heart does not try to operate the respiratory system, nor does the brain try to operate the circulatory system, but the heart and the brain do what they have been created to do for the normal functioning of the body. So must all the members of Christ's Body find and function in what they were created for.

> *For the body is not one member, but many. If the foot shall say, Because I am not the hand, I am not of the body; is it therefore not of the body? And if the ear shall say, Because I am not the eye, I am not of the body; is it therefore not of the body? If the whole body were an eye, where were the hearing? If the whole were hearing, where were the smelling? But now hath God set the members every one of them in the body, as it hath pleased him.*     1 Corinthians 12:14-18

There must be unity in the Body. In the physical body, the head cannot be separated from the body and maintain life. Nor can any part of limb be separated from the Body and live. In the same manner, we cannot be separated from Christ or from one another. The Lord Jesus has put us in this Body in complete union.

The various parts of the physical body do not need to think to coordinate the activity of the body. Some will interact through relationship, but their instructions all come from the head. The left foot and the right foot do not have direct communication; it is the head that coordinates the movements of both of them. The hands do not order the eyes to see or look. The head gives command to the eyes in dreams, visions, and revelations.

The members of Christ's Body are subject to one another. None can claim superiority of purpose or function. We may interact through relationship, but we must receive our directions and instructions from Christ, the Head, and His chief administrator, the Holy Spirit.

The physical body also shares some similar things that separate it from all other bodies. Every part of the physical body has the same blood running through it and every part shares the same DNA. These two things identify body parts as belonging to the same body.

All the parts of the Body of Christ also share the same blood—the blood of Christ, and we are imprinted with the same DNA—the Holy Spirit. Through these two things, we are identifiable as the Body of Christ.

# 8 - Who Needs Whom?

Teamwork and cooperation are essential in the Body. Each member must work together with the rest for the good of the whole Body. A one-man show doesn't get very far here. God designed each member of the Body to fit within the whole, and each is dependent upon the others.

*So we, being many, are one body in Christ, and every one members one of another. Having then gifts differing according to the grace that is given to us, whether prophecy, let us prophesy according to the proportion of faith; or ministry, let us wait on our ministering: or he that teacheth, on teaching; or he that exhorteth, on exhortation: he that giveth, let him do it with simplicity; he that ruleth, with diligence; he that showeth mercy, with cheerfulness. Let love be without dissimulation. Abhor that which is evil; cleave to that which is good. Be kindly affectioned one to another with brotherly love; in honour preferring one another.*
Romans 12:5-10

*And if they were all one member, where were the body? But now are they many members, yet but one body. And the eye cannot say unto the hand, I have no need of thee: nor again the head to the feet, I have no need of you. Nay, much more those members of the body, which seem to be more feeble, are necessary: and those members of the body, which we think to be less honourable, upon these we bestow more abundant honour; and our uncomely parts have more abundant comeliness. For our comely parts have no need: but God hath tempered the body together, having given more abundant honour to that part which lacked: that there should be no schism in the body; but that the members should have the same care one for another. And whether one member suffer, all the members suffer with it; or one member be honoured, all the members rejoice with it. Now ye are the body of Christ, and members in particular.*         1 Corinthians 12:19-27

There is a parallel between the natural and the spiritual. The human body is composed of many parts, each performing a different function, and each equally important for the normal functioning of the human body. The eyes cannot hear for the ears, nor the ears pump blood for the heart. The hands cannot perform for the nose. In order for the body to operate in perfection, each part must be in full operation. A machine can also be likened to the human body. When all the parts of the machine are functioning as they have been designed to, the machine fulfills its purpose. If a bolt or screw is out of place or missing, the machine will become inoperative or unable to reach its maximum potential.

Just as each part or member of the human body does not have to stop and take note or examine what the other part of the body does, likewise each member of the Body of Christ must operate in the specific office or capacity they have been called to by their Head.

> *But I would have you know, that the head of every man is Christ.*                 1 Corinthians 11:3

Jesus Christ is the Head of the Body, the Church. He is the beginning, the firstborn from the dead, that in all things He might have the preeminence.

> *And he is the head of the body, the church: who is the beginning, the firstborn from the dead; that in all things he might have the preeminence. For it pleased the Father that in him should all fulness dwell.*
> Colossians 1:18-19

In the natural body, the head houses the brain which can be thought of as the control center, or computer, of the body. The brain receives signals from other parts of the body, adds them up, and signals back for action, within a split second. The brain enables man to have sensations, to make judgments, to initiate actions, and to think creatively. The body receives its instructions from the brain. This aptly illustrates the relationship between Christ and the Church.

The Church, the Body of Christ, is a body of believers united organically with one another by the baptizing work of the Holy Spirit. The Body of Christ is composed of many members and systems. This organism is made up of members of all denominations, even as the natural body is composed of many members and systems.

The framework that holds the human body together is the skeleton. The skeleton is made mostly of bones. Bones fit together at joints and are held fast by tough cords called ligaments. Some joints can be moved freely, while others cannot be moved at all. When you run, you move your legs at the knee and hip joints. When you throw a ball, you move your arm at the shoulder and elbow joints. You can move your spine, but not too freely. In the base of the spine the bones are fused, forming one bony plate that fits into another. Neither moves. The joints in your skull are solid, except for those in the jaw. The skeleton does two main jobs. It supports the body. It also protects the delicate internal organs.

Like the skeleton, Jesus is our support system in the Body of Christ. He says,

> *...Without me ye can do nothing.*      John 15:5

A joint is the point of contact between moving parts of a skeleton. It has other parts that surround and support it. Every part in the Body of Christ is fitly joined together with each other part through Jesus.

The Body of Christ is not centered around one "joint" (one denomination, one church, one ministry), but every member of the Body doing its part will ensure the effectual working, or proper functioning, of the whole Body.

Bones are the framework in the human body, but they cannot move themselves. Muscles are the body movers. For every bone that can move, there are muscles to move it. A muscle moves a bone by pulling it. Muscles are firmly anchored to the bones by hard tendons. Muscles pull but they cannot push, so they must work in pairs. To do the work, muscles must burn fuel. The fuel for humans is the food they eat.

> *But some man will say, How are the dead raised up? and with what body do they come? Thou fool, that which thou sowest is not quickened, except it die: and that which thou sowest, thou sowest not that body that shall be, but bare grain, it may chance of wheat, or of some other grain: but God giveth it a body as it hath pleased him, and to every seed his own body.... So also is the resurrection of the dead. It is sown in corruption; it is raised in incorruption: it is sown in dishonour; it is raised in glory: it is sown in weakness; it is raised in power: it is sown a natural body; it is raised a spiritual body. There is a natural body, and there is a spiritual body.*  1 Corinthians 15:35-38, 42-44

In the natural body, the back is very different from the front. But the two sides are exactly alike. Each side has an eye, ear, arm, leg and lung. Humans have a two-sided body plan. One side is a mirror image of the other. The same is true of our natural body and our spiritual body. One is a mirror image of the other.

The Body of Christ is a living, breathing body on earth that is massive and widespread. It extends from earth to Heaven, and it grew from a tiny seed in the womb of a woman. The Head of that Body is seated in Heaven on the right hand of the Father. In the seat of power and authority, Christ has authority in Heaven, and He has delegated authority on earth to His Body, the Church.

We are the Body of Christ, and we are coming into the knowledge that we are in Christ and He is in us. We are also being awakened to our division and disconnection from one another in the Body and to our lack of awareness of and sensitivity to one another because we have been so denomination and organization conscious. Like Adam, we can now say of the other members of the Body that they are bone of our bones and flesh of our flesh. And like Paul, we can confess:

> *So we, being many, are one body in Christ, and every one members one of another.*     Romans 12:5

When one member of the Body suffers, the others should also feel that suffering. When one member is honored, all the other members should rejoice with it. (See 1 Corinthians 12:26.)

Suffering is a sensation and so is rejoicing. Your senses are windows and through them you learn. Information comes in to you through your eyes, ears, nose, tongue, and skin. No sense works alone. We do not see with our eyes alone or hear only with our ears. The senses are reporters. Not until the message reaches the brain do we actually see, hear, smell, taste or feel.

*Who Needs Whom?*

If my little toe hurts, my whole body knows it and is affected by it. Whatever happens to us as a spiritual body (the Body of Christ) affects us all. Inasmuch as my toe is hurting, my foot knows it, my leg knows it, and the other members of my body know it, because the brain has received the message, processed it, and notified the rest of the body. If the apostle, prophet, evangelist, pastor, or teacher hurts, so do the other members of the Body.

The senses alone do not tell us anything. They are reporters, and what they report must travel along the nerves to the brain before it means anything. When the brain receives a report, it decides what action to take, if any.

The brain is located in the head and Christ is the Head of the Body. The brain gets the signals, adds them up, and signals back for action within a split second. We receive our signals from the Holy Spirit who lives in us.

Sensing, putting together, and responding are the jobs of the nervous system. The nervous system is made up of the brain, the spinal cord, and the nerves. Different parts of the brain do different things. Could we correlate this the work of the Holy Spirit?

There are receptors for every sensation. A receptor is an organ, such as the eye or the ear that has sensitive nerve endings. The eye is like a camera that constantly adjusts itself to take and develop an endless stream of pictures. Should you have an artificial eye, it may appear to be almost the same as the real eye; nevertheless, it has no sight in it. Similarly, when members of the Body suffer, other members will have no awareness of this because there is no sight in it. Body consciousness enables you to know spontaneously without the need of being told. The

Body of Christ has been given gifts of the Spirit to help us know the condition of the Body and what action should be taken—the gifts of prophecy, faith, the word of knowledge, the word of wisdom, tongues, interpretation of tongues, gifts of healing, working of miracles.

In the ear, sounds are caused by vibrations of the tiny hairs that line the insides of the ear canal. You can hear because your ears detect these vibrations and report them to your brain. You cannot see sounds, but sometimes you can feel them through vibrations. The ears bring you both warning and pleasure, and also serve as organs for learning. In Christ's Body, we have received God's DNA. We are also spirit beings and have the ability to hear God as He speaks to us in various ways, whether in His Word, in dreams and visions, in nature, or in revelation.

Even in the natural body's systems of defense, we see how the Body of Christ is meant to operate. The natural body's systems work together for the health of the entire body. The Body of Christ must also work together in harmony and unity to keep the whole healthy. The Holy Spirit helps to bring balance in the Body. He is our doctor, nurse, nutritionist, and pharmacist all rolled into one. He is sent to guide us into all truth, and the Word of God is our guidebook which provides the nutrients and the diet plan we need to stay healthy.

The natural body protects itself against disease-causing microorganisms by the formation of antibodies. Even as the natural body comes to its own defense when disease or bacteria enter and antibodies are formed and sent to confront the invaders as members of the Body of Christ, we too must become antibodies and white blood cells, engulfing bacteria and toxins and causing them to be removed from the Body. The bacteria of an evil tongue, lying, gossiping, judging, criticizing, backbiting, envy, false doctrine, strife, and division must be removed from the Body to keep it healthy. Prayer and intercession are important tools in uprooting the works of darkness, and discipleship enforces accountability.

We could go on and on with the comparisons between the physical body and the Body of Christ. With the description of each body part, you will most likely think of a fellow believer, or a group of believers, who may fill that same function in the Body.

The senses of taste and smell are closely related and work together. The nerve cells of the skin are scattered all over the body. The circulatory system provides protection to the body from loss of blood and from disease. As you examine how a physical body operates, you gain a clear idea of how Christ's spiritual Body functions.

Picture a drawing of the Body of Christ, and the image you conjure up may look something like this:

*And God hath set some in the church, first apostles, secondarily prophets, thirdly teachers, after that miracles, then gifts of healings, helps, governments, diversities of tongues. Are all apostles? are all prophets? are all teachers? are all workers of miracles?*
1 Corinthians 12:28-29

*And he gave some, apostles; and some, prophets; and*

*some, evangelists; and some, pastors and teachers; for the perfecting of the saints, for the work of the ministry, for the edifying of the body of Christ: till we all come in the unity of the faith, and of the knowledge of the Son of God, unto a perfect man, unto the measure of the stature of the fulness of Christ: that we henceforth be no more children, tossed to and fro, and carried about with every wind of doctrine, by the sleight of men, and cunning craftiness, whereby they lie in wait to deceive; but speaking the truth in love, may grow up into him in all things, which is the head, even Christ: from whom the whole body fitly joined together and compacted by that which every joint supplieth, according to the effectual working in the measure of every part, maketh increase of the body unto the edifying of itself in love.* Ephesians 4:11-16

# 9 – Governing Body

*Know ye not that ye are the temple of God, and that the Spirit of God dwelleth in you?*
                                                1 Corinthians 3:16

The Body of Christ is a governing Body. This is so because all authority in Heaven and on earth rests upon Jesus' shoulders, and He has given that authority to us, His Body, because we are His representatives here on earth. The governing Body of Christ consists of the members who know and understand how the spiritual realm works and who operate in that authority. Christ has released in His Body His life and His rulership to be lived out in the earth.

## The Ministry Gifts

The authority as ordained by the Lord is seen in His gifts to the Body.

*But unto every one of us is given grace according to the*

> *measure of the gift of Christ. Wherefore he saith, When he ascended up on high, he led captivity captive, and gave gifts unto men. ...And he gave some, apostles; and some, prophets; and some, evangelists; and some, pastors and teachers; for the perfecting of the saints, for the work of the ministry, for the edifying of the body of Christ.* Ephesians 4:7-8, 11-12

Apostles, prophets, evangelists, pastors, and teachers are the five-fold ministry gifts Christ gave to the Church to govern the Body of Christ and to equip it for ministry. These gifts are often called the hand ministry, and it is supported by the ministry of helps. Each of these gifts is a finger in the hand.

The apostle is the finger that points both inward and outward. He is one who is sent.

The prophet is the finger that points the way in which the Spirit is leading, presenting God's will to the people.

The evangelist is the longest finger. He or she can reach farther and through signs, wonders, and miracles to bring people to God.

The pastor is the ring finger, which represents the unending cycle of life. He is the nurturer. He cares for the ones appointed to his fold. He uses the rod to lead them in the ways of God.

The teacher is the little finger. This finger is tiny enough to get into the smallest of places. This means the teacher has the ability to plant truth and to pull out and dig out untruth, even in difficult places.

## *Mirror Images*

Much can be learned from viewing the plan of the natural body of man. In the natural body, your back is very different from your front, but your two sides are exactly alike. One side is a mirror image of the other side. They are identical except that they are opposites. The same is true of the spiritual Body of Christ. There are two sides to the Body. We look back to Israel, God's chosen people, which is our foundation, our root, and we can see one side of the Body. Jesus came through the lineage of King David and is rooted in that royal line. Jesus came to Israel to bring redemption, but was rejected by Israel, who knew Him not. This redemption was then taken to the Gentiles who did not know about the prophecies concerning a Messiah, but the Gentiles accepted Him, and the bloodline of God's family passed on to everyone who accepts Jesus as Savior.

We can also see mirror images in looking at the first man, Adam, and at Christ. The first man, Adam, is one side of the image and is very different from the second Adam, Christ, who is the other side of the image, but is Adam's opposite. Man's relationship with God was severed by the first Adam, but it was restored by the second Adam, who is Christ.

God originally gave all authority on earth to the first Adam. God said to the first Adam:

> *Be fruitful, and multiply, and replenish the earth, and subdue it: and have dominion over the fish of the sea,*

*and over the fowl of the air, and over every living thing that moveth upon the earth.* Genesis 1:28

The first Adam, a being of earthly origin, had dominion over the fish, the fowl, and all of the living creatures that moved upon the earth. This Adam lost his authority to Satan when he disobeyed God.

Christ, the second Adam, also received all authority in both Heaven and earth, but He received it as a result of His obedience to God. Christ is a quickening spirit of heavenly origin. This second Adam had the task of reconciling man back to God, restoring God's family, and enforcing the righteous rule of God on earth.

These two images of Adam are alike in the sense that both had their brides taken from their sides. Adam received his bride after he fell into a deep sleep and the rib was taken from his body to create woman. The Hebrew word for *rib* means, "of the body." When the woman was brought to Adam, he declared of her, *"This is now bone of my bones, and flesh of my flesh: she shall be called Woman, because she was taken out of Man"* (Genesis 2:23).

The birthing of Christ's bride began in the piercing of His side in death when blood and water, which are the substance of life, poured out of Him.

## The Structure of Authority

The Body of Christ is structured to function as a corporation. ***Merriam-Webster's Dictionary*** describes a *corporation* as "a body formed and authorized the law to act as a single person although constituted by one or more persons and legally endowed with rights and duties including the capacity of succession."

A corporation operates on a set of bylaws. A *bylaw* is "a rule adopted by an organization chiefly for the government of its members and the regulation of its affairs." Similarly, the Body of Christ also has rules of conduct, which were taught by Jesus in His Sermon on the Mount.

All corporations have a structure of authority. As the Creator, God has determined the structure of authority on the earth. We see the initiation of authority in the Garden of Eden. God gave Adam authority to keep the Garden. Adam had dominion, or rule, over the fish of the sea, over the fowl of the air, and over everything that moved upon the earth. After Adam's fall into disobedience, his authority had to be redefined. He no longer had dominion over the creatures. The earth would no longer freely give its increase to him. Instead, he had to work and sweat to get the earth to produce. He was given rule over the woman. This authority over his household is reiterated in the New Covenant.

> *For the husband is the head of the wife, even as Christ is the head of the church.*     Ephesians 5:23

As the wife is subject to her husband, she is obedient to the delegated authority of God, which God Himself vested in the man as head of his household.

Children are subject to the authority of their parents, which is delegated by God.

*Children, obey your parents in the Lord: for this is right. Honour thy father and mother; which is the first commandment with promise; that it may be well with thee, and thou mayest live long on the earth.*

Ephesians 6:1-3

Servants are subject to the authority of their masters. In our culture, this applies to the definitions of employees and employers as well.

*Servants, be obedient to them that are your masters according to the flesh, with fear and trembling, in singleness of your heart, as unto Christ; not with eyeservice, as menpleasers; but as the servants of Christ, doing the will of God from the heart; with good will doing service, as to the Lord, and not to men: knowing that whatsoever good thing any man doeth, the same shall he receive of the Lord, whether he be bond or free.*

Ephesians 6:5-8

And masters are instructed on how to handle their authority over their servants.

*And, ye masters, do the same things unto them, forbearing threatening: knowing that your Master also is in heaven; neither is there respect of persons with him.*

Ephesians 6:9

Just as God has structured authority in the family and in the work setting, He has also set authority in the

Church, the Body of Christ. God has given the governing, operation, and execution of His purpose and plans for the Body to the fivefold ministry—apostles, prophets, evangelists, pastors, and teachers. They are set under the divine authority of Christ.

Authority in the world is imperfect. As individuals, we are subject to the misuse of authority; for example, governments sometimes misuse authority and make wrong decisions. *Submission*, "yielding oneself to the authority or will of another," is also imperfect in this world. If it wasn't, then there would be no need for prisons. God's structure of authority and submission as it relates to Christ and the Body, however, is perfect when everyone involved adheres to it as God's Word directs.

Situations do sometimes occur where our relationships with others are severed. This can happen between servants and masters, employees and bosses, parents and children, husbands and wives, pastors and their congregations, or anywhere that a structure of authority exists. In these instances, it is not God's structure that has failed—it is the people involved who have not yielded to the structure of authority. If the child is abused, the parent has not wielded authority properly. If the congregation is misled, the pastor has not used his God-given authority correctly. If a husband deserts his wife, the husband has rejected the authority of Christ over him. Only when we all obey God's structure of authority does it work perfectly. But we should not ever reject God's structure of authority simply because some people fail to obey it.

In the natural body, the head cannot be separated from

the body and maintain life; the two must remain as one. In the same manner, Christ and the Church cannot be severed—they are one Body, with many members in different locations, but connected one to another.

We can observe how authority operates in the natural body. There are many members in the natural body: the sense organs, muscles, glands, lungs, heart, liver, bladder, stomach, intestines, cells and tissues. There are also many systems in the natural body: the circulatory system, respiratory system, digestive system, waste-disposal system, heating and cooling system. These must work in cooperation with one another. Each member performs the function that has been assigned to it. Therefore, there must be coordination in the body. Instruction must come from somewhere. In the natural body, instruction and direction come from the head, or the brain.

The members of the body are subject to the authority of the head. The left foot and the right foot do not have a conversation; the head sends out the signals through the nerves to the proper muscles to move both feet in the necessary way to walk. The eyes do not order the hands to grasp; the head receives information from the eyes and then gives the command to the hands. All the members of the body have the same relationship with the head within the structure of authority. No member is more special than the others. All are necessary for the proper functioning of the body and all must follow the structure of authority for the body to work as it was designed to work.

It's no different in the Body of Christ. Each member is subject to the authority of Christ. The function of each member is limited to the authority given it by Christ. Whatever a member does is attributed to Christ, and the glory belongs to God.

It is Christ who commands the prophet to "see" and how to communicate what is seen. It is Christ who directs the work of the ministry. It is Christ who sends the evangelist forth to preach the Gospel, though not his or her gospel—Christ's Gospel.

Sometimes an injury may occur in the natural body so that a limb or an organ is not functioning properly. Other parts may for a time perform in the place of that injured part, but can't really take the place of that part. But then healing takes place, and that part of the body is not rejected but restored to its proper functioning.

We see this same principle in operation in the Body of Christ. We ought not to refuse the function of any member, for each member is gifted for a unique purpose and function within the Body. When a member of the Body falls into error, repents, and turns back to God, we are not to reject that member, but rather we are to restore him to his rightful place. To reject another member of the Body of Christ is the same as rejecting the authority of Christ. If a fallen member has repented and is healed, Christ restores him to his proper place in the Body. To reject that member is to be in disobedience to the authority of Christ.

Not only should we accept that member back in, but it is also our responsibility to come alongside fallen members for the purpose of helping to restore them. It is said that geese fly in a V-formation because this gives them greater lift power. They fly best as a unified group. If one goose falls out, two others will follow it down to assist. Who gives them this command? Shouldn't we follow such an example?

In the natural body, there are members that hold authority over other parts, such as the nerve endings and the muscles. The head sends signals down through the nerve, which command the muscles to move organs and limbs. The nerve and muscles receive their authority from the head and move solely at the direction of the head. The foot cannot reject the commands of the muscles that move it without rejecting the authority of the head itself.

The same is true in the Body of Christ. There are also members of the Body who hold God-given authority over other members, such as the apostle, prophet, evangelist, pastor, and teacher. These individuals may in turn give authority to others within the Body to direct and instruct the members. For example, a pastor may empower a member to serve as the head of a committee, or the apostle may empower a pastor under his authority to plant a church. If we accept the authority God has given to His designated leadership, it is the same as accepting the authority of Christ.

We are to be in fellowship and harmony, working together in unity. One member is not the whole Body. One church or denomination is not the whole Body. We must learn to stand in the position of being a member and accepting the work of all the members. If a member is gifted to see in the Spirit or hear from God, that becomes my way of seeing and hearing also if I am not gifted to see or hear for myself.

## The Power of Unity

No member can afford to be independent of the Body. Just as a limb that is cut from a tree will soon wither and die, we too will become dead and dry if we are cut off from the Body.

We are not to forsake the assembling of ourselves together as stated in Hebrews 10:25. *To assemble* means, "to put together, to put in working order or operation." A single horsepower in an automobile engine is of little good to move the thousands of pounds in an automobile. Half of the potential horsepower will operate the vehicle weakly, but not at full capacity. It takes the full horsepower designed into the engine to move a machine that size and fulfill its potential. We as a corporate Body have much power. Let us assemble together to do the great works that Christ spoke of before He ascended to the right hand of the Father.

> *He that believeth on me, the works that I do shall he do also; and greater works than these shall he do; because I go unto my Father.* John 14:12

Let us not be the one who desires to be the all-in-all. If we are gifted to serve in the ministry of helps, we should not try to do the work of the apostle, nor attempt to see for the prophet, nor should we shepherd for the pastor. Let us not break ranks. The authority given to the offices of ministry is not given to oppress, trouble, hinder, or bind, but rather it is given to build according to God's divine plan in order to accomplish God's plan and purpose on earth.

The Body needs the apostles, the prophets, the evangelists, the pastors, and the teachers. But it also needs the intercessors, the prayer warriors, the exhorters, the helpers, the givers, and all the other parts. The ministry is not yours, mine, the denomination's, or the assembly's—it is Christ's, and every part is subject to Him.

If you are gifted for an office of ministry, don't withhold what you've been given from the Body. You are equipped for leadership, so lead! To the apostle, go where you are sent with the message and mission of Christ. You have been anointed for leadership, government, and organizational skills. Build, as Christ leads.

To the prophet, give the message. Prophesy whether in words, deed, prophetic life, or prophetic action. Point the way. Show us when, how, and where the Spirit is moving.

To the evangelist, preach the Gospel. Preach whether they will receive it or will not receive it. Go equipped with signs, wonders, and miracles confirming the Word.

To the pastor, feed the lambs. Feed the sheep. Care for them. Examine your flock in prayer and intercession, and if a "tick" is found, pour in the oil until the tick backs out. Feed them, lead them, and teach them.

To the teacher, teach them how to rightly divide the Word of truth. Open up the Word to them and give them the revelation of the Word.

To the one gifted to serve in other ways, don't withhold those gifts just because you are not gifted with an office. You are just as vital as any office.

To the intercessor, give spiritual birth. Watch as well as pray. Engage in prophetic intercession, wage warfare, and watch for the Body.

To the helper, work the works of Christ and offer help where needed.

To the giver, meet the needs of the Body when and where they exist. Provide for evangelism, missions, and the everyday needs of the Body.

To all the members, stay in constant communion and fellowship with the Holy Spirit and with our Lord and Savior. Worship God.

Just as the physical body is unified through its genetic makeup, so also the Body of Christ is genetically linked. *Genetic linkage* is "a relationship between two or more genes occupying the same chromosome that causes or connects one part of the body with another." We are genetically linked to Christ and to each other. The Holy Spirit, our spiritual DNA, unifies us as one Body that is directed by the authority of the Head.

## Authority Over Darkness

As a governing Body, our conflict with darkness is like a wrestling match. The Scriptures tell us that we are not wrestling with *"flesh and blood, but against principalities, against powers, against the rulers of the darkness of this world, against spiritual wickedness in high places"* (Ephesians 6:12).

These spirits of darkness are causing a great deal of mental, emotional, and spiritual harm as they work from their place in the second heaven against the Body of Christ. These spirits delight in working through some denominations, assemblies, and religious organizations by separating them from the truth of the Word of God and causing them to work contrary to the Kingdom of God.

*These Bones Will Live*

The Holy Spirit is issuing a call in this day for the Body to rise up in strength and take its place of authority to oppose the darkness. Religious systems and denominational walls have bound parts of the Body, and the Spirit is beginning to break down these barriers to truth. The Body is beginning to experience a renewed commitment to the mission of Christ in this hour.

Darkness is being transmitted into our homes daily by way of television and radio, which infiltrates the minds of our youth, men and women. The antichrist spirit seeks to spoil our children. Right is portrayed as wrong and wrong behavior is seen as right. This has brought moral decay into our society.

But the Body is now rising and shaking itself free from the filth and garbage of the world. Let us as believers in Christ begin to sound the alarm against these evil spirits and loose them from their habitations. Let us protect our children from media witchcraft, which is designed to indoctrinate our children at an early age through cartoons, books, and toys. Let us sound the alarm.

> *Blow ye the trumpet in Zion, and sound an alarm in my holy mountain: let all the inhabitants of the land tremble: for the day of the LORD cometh, for it is nigh at hand.*     Joel 2:1

The Body is waking from a drug-induced sleep. We have been drugged by the cares of the world and carnality, but now we are being released in the power and anointing to destroy the yokes of bondage. We are realizing the authority we carry in the name of Jesus Christ. We are being revitalized and reinvigorated and we are now proclaiming:

> *The Spirit of the Lord is upon me* [the body], *because he hath anointed me* [the body] *to preach the gospel to the poor; he hath sent me* [the body] *to heal the brokenhearted, to preach deliverance to the captives, and recovering of sight to the blind, to set at liberty them that are bruised, To preach the acceptable year of the Lord.* Luke 4:18-19

Of the two spiritual forces in the world today, the greater One is in the Body. The Holy Spirit resides in the Body. Through the leading of the Spirit, we are discovering the authority that we hold, and learning how to tear down the works of the enemy.

> *How can one enter into a strong man's house, and spoil his goods, except he first bind the strong man? and then he will spoil his house.* Matthew 12:29

The word *strongman* comes from the Greek word *ischuros*, and it refers to "one who rules by brute force." This is the type of power demons bring with them when they afflict men. Jesus spoke of entering the house of the strongman and spoiling his goods. *Spoil* is from the Greek word *diarpazō*, meaning, "to tear in pieces, to dismantle, to snatch from, to seize as plunder."

God's Word tells us in 1 John 3:8 that one of the main purposes Jesus came was to *"destroy the works of the devil."*

He was given the authority and power to do this, and because we are His Body, we now have the same purpose and power. After His crucifixion, Christ went down into hell (see Ephesians 4:9) and took the keys of death and hell from Satan (see Revelation 1:18). He spoiled the enemy's house and set the captives free. As His Body, we are equipped to do the same.

> *For though we walk in the flesh, we do not war after the flesh: (for the weapons of our warfare are not carnal, but mighty through God to the pulling down of strong holds;).* 2 Corinthians 10:3-4

## Authority to Preach

Because we are a governing Body, Christ has commissioned us to go forth in His authority to share the Gospel with the whole world.

> *Go ye into all the world, and preach the gospel to every creature. He that believeth and is baptized shall be saved; but he that believeth not shall be damned. And these signs shall follow them that believe; In my name shall they cast out devils; they shall speak with new tongues; they shall take up serpents; and if they drink any deadly thing, it shall not hurt them; they shall lay hands on the sick, and they shall recover.*
> Mark 16:15-18

The word *preach* comes from the Greek word *kerusso*. It means, "to proclaim as a herald, to cry as a conqueror, announce publicly."

Jesus told His Body to announce publicly that the

Kingdom of Heaven was at hand, and then to demonstrate the power of the Kingdom by healing the sick, cleansing the lepers, casting out demons, and raising the dead.

## The Revival of Authority

Today, alignment is taking place in the Body. The Holy Spirit is in the midst of the Body applying oil and wine, working the work of His ministry in the Body. For centuries we have been disjoined, but now we are being fitly joined together. The Spirit is calling each member to take his or her respective place. Our Head is directing us to come together in unity and stand firm. There is no room for anyone to be out of place. No one should break ranks under the governing authority of the Head of the Body.

A change has come to the Church. Revival fires are aglow all over the world. The glory of the Lord is filling the land through His Body, the light of the world. The prophet Joel said:

> *And it shall come to pass afterward, that I will pour out my spirit upon all flesh; and your sons and your daughters shall prophesy, your old men shall dream dreams, your young men shall see visions: and also upon the servants and upon the handmaids in those days will I pour out my spirit.* Joel 2:28-29

The Body has been going through a period of purification, in which the oil of myrrh is being applied. The bent frames of our minds are being straightened, all the filth in our souls is being purged, and our human spirits are being cleansed of all the fears, emotional scars, bruises, and wounds that have victimized us for so many years. We once again see deliverance ministries coming forth to set the captives free.

Many in the Body are wondering what is happening in their lives as the Father works a work of holiness and character building in them. The old ways of seeing things, and the walls and partitions of iniquity that have separated members from Him are being torn down. A lack of teaching is being replaced with the solid foundation of the apostles and prophets. The work of restoration of the ministry of the apostles and prophets is bringing much light to the Body. The ministry offices are no longer erased from the minds of members who once said, "There are no more apostles and prophets."

The ordained order of the Body is being restored. The unity that Christ prayed for among His people is being manifested. The proper function of authority is being resurrected. There is no question as to why this is happening, for God makes the purpose clear in His Word:

> *...for the perfecting of the saints, for the work of the ministry, for the edifying of the body of Christ: till we all come in the unity of the faith, and of the knowledge of the Son of God, unto a perfect man, unto the measure of the stature of the fulness of Christ.*
> Ephesians 4:12-13

This scripture says, *"till we all come unto a perfect man,"*—not a perfect man individually, but a perfect man as a Body. We must be healed and functioning in the order in which we were created to function—not dismantled or dismembered, but whole and totally restored.

The Holy Spirit is the chief administrator in the Body, and He is at work today bringing us into the unity of the faith. Jesus said of the Holy Spirit:

> *...I tell you the truth; It is expedient for you that I go away: for if I go not away, the Comforter will not come unto you; but if I depart, I will send him unto you. And when he is come, he will reprove the world of sin, and of righteousness, and of judgment: of sin, because they believe not on me; of righteousness, because I go to my Father, and ye see me no more; of judgment, because the prince of this world is judged.... Howbeit when he, the Spirit of truth, is come, he will guide you into all truth: for he shall not speak of himself; but whatsoever he shall hear, that shall he speak: and he will show you things to come.* John 16:7-11,13

As we are healed, restored, and united, we will come into the fullness of the authority Christ has vested in us, so that we may govern as God originally intended at the creation of the world.

# 10 – Behold, the Bridegroom Cometh

The Body of Christ has a second identity, which is the Bride of Christ. In this hour, the Bride is beginning her work of purification in preparation for the wedding. At the arrival of the Bridegroom, the Bride must be without blemish. She must be free from moral guilt. As the Bride increases her purifying, she will increase in her freedom from all that has made her weak and ineffective.

Since the time of the fall of man, the human race's ability to grasp truth has been hindered. Our understanding has been darkened and our perception of life and its priorities has been distorted. The Bride of Christ is a spiritual being who exists in the natural realm. She has for centuries been deceived into believing she is limited by the natural effects of the fall. Trespass and sin have dulled her conscience, contaminated her emotions, weakened her will, and made her mind unable to think straight. Only as she works through the purification process will she find release from those things that have bound her.

The apostle Paul had a passion to see the Bride of Christ mature into all God has called her to be. He prayed that we, the Bride, would find wisdom:

> *...that the God of our Lord Jesus Christ, the Father of glory, may give unto you the spirit of wisdom and revelation in the knowledge of him.* Ephesians 1:17

> *For this cause we also, since the day we heard it, do not cease to pray for you, and to desire that ye might be filled with the knowledge of his will in all wisdom and spiritual understanding.* Colossians 1:9

He also prayed that we, the Bride of Christ, would be strengthened:

> *...that he would grant you, according to the riches of his glory, to be strengthened with might by his Spirit in the inner man.* Ephesians 3:16

Furthermore, he prayed:

> *...that ye might walk worthy of the Lord unto all pleasing, being fruitful in every good work, and increasing in the knowledge of God.* Colossians 1:10

The Bride of Christ is awakening and yielding to the Holy Spirit to be purified. Her thoughts are centered on her hope.

> *When he shall appear, we shall be like him; for we*

> *shall see him as he is. And every man that hath this hope in him purifieth himself, even as he is pure.*
> 1 John 3:2,3

She will be free from that which corrupts. She will be free from all that does not belong to or have a right to be in her. She will be free from fault and guilt. She will be clean and untainted with worldly elements.

As the Bride grows in the knowledge of Christ's love for her, she will be able to show forth His love to others. This, in turn, will awaken a desire within others to find Him in His fullness.

If you read Song of Solomon 5:4-8, you will be touched by the bride's sense of neglect of service, and then by the change that begins to take place within. She begins to awaken and respond to her bridegroom's desires.

Her ultimate response can be summed up as follows:

> *Many waters cannot quench love, neither can the floods drown it.* Song of Solomon 8:7

It is now the bridegroom himself who occupies her heart, not a desire for personal comfort. His desires are now her desires. She will now work *"joined unto the Lord as one spirit"* (see 1 Corinthians 6:17), bone of his bones, flesh of his flesh—his Body.

The Bride of Christ is putting on the garment of fine linen, which is the righteous works of godliness and goodness produced by the Holy Spirit. This is accomplished as she judges her flesh and yields herself to God.

*But put ye on the Lord Jesus Christ, and make not provision for the flesh, to fulfil the lusts thereof.*
Romans 13:14

The Bride shall now adorn herself with the good works for which she is created in Christ Jesus (see Ephesians 2:10), that she may bring honor to His name.

*Having your conversation honest among the Gentiles: that, whereas they speak against you as evildoers, they may by your good works, which they shall behold, glorify God in the day of visitation.* 1 Peter 2:12

The Bride is awakened and alert to the Bridegroom's soon return for her. She wants to be ready for this celebration. Therefore, she recognizes that tests and trials lie ahead of her. She will be tested at the point of her faithful and loyal service to the Bridegroom, her Master. And she will be rewarded accordingly.

The Church is like the bride described in Song of Solomon 2:14. She is His dove. In herself, she has faults, but if found in Him, she is blameless and harmless, for this is the character of the dove.

*Behold the bridegroom cometh; go ye out to meet him.*
Matthew 25:6

# 11 – A Gentile Bride

Joshua had delivered God's people to the Promised Land. The Law had been given and the priesthood had been established. Provision had been made for the covering of the sins of God's people through sacrificial offerings, paving the way for God's final sacrifice for sin. The redemption of man was approaching.

It is in this setting that the book of Ruth takes place. The book of Ruth tells the story of Ruth and Boaz, and it foreshadows the redemption of all the Gentile nations. In this story, Boaz redeems Elimelech's, Chilion's, and Mahlon's inheritance in order to raise up the name of the dead so that their names would not be cut off and their lineage would not end.

To understand, let's look at the story from the beginning, and as we go, let's also consider the parallels to the Body of Christ.

Elimelech and his wife, Naomi, and two sons, Mahlon and Chilion left Bethlehem in Judah because of a famine and went to live in Moab. While living in Moab, Elimelech died, leaving Naomi in the care of their two sons. These sons both took Moabite women for their wives. Unfortunately, both sons died ten years later. Neither of these sons had sired any heirs during their marriages.

Naomi, now left alone with only her two daughters-in-law, heard that the famine in Judah had ended, and she decided to return there from Moab. Naomi advised her daughters-in-law to return to their families. One of her daughters-in-law, Orpah, returned to her family, but Ruth did not want to return to her family or stay in Moab. Ruth, as a Moabitess, was a Gentile. She is a type of the Church, or the Body of Christ.

So Ruth made a vow to follow Naomi back to Bethlehem-judah and to accept the God of Israel as her God. Ruth told her mother-in-law:

> *Entreat me not to leave thee, or to return from following after thee: for whither thou goest, I will go; and where thou lodgest, I will lodge: thy people shall be my people, and thy God my God: where thou diest, will I die, and there will I be buried: the LORD do so to me, and more also, if ought but death part thee and me.*
> Ruth 1:16,17

Once in Judah, Ruth needed to provide for herself and Naomi. Ruth went out to glean in the harvest fields for the purpose of obtaining food for herself and her mother-in-law, Naomi. The Levitical law stated that the gleanings of the harvest must be left for the poor. *To glean* means, "to pick up after a reaper." There is also another meaning for the word *glean*. It means, "to gather information or other material bit by bit." Bit by bit Ruth picked up information concerning the kinsman-redeemer. It was by chance that Ruth gleaned in the field belonging to Boaz, who was Elimelech's kinsman. Boaz is a type of Christ, our Redeemer.

Boaz was very kind to Ruth. Ruth was told to keep close to Boaz's maidens and never be found in another field. The Church must stay close to Christ, the Head, and not be found to be partakers of the things of the world.

Naomi sought a better life for Ruth, so she instructed Ruth on how to arrange a marriage with her kinsman, Boaz. Naomi explained to her the customs she must follow to have Boaz claim the right of kinsman-redeemer. Under Levitical law, when a man died childless, his brother was bound to raise up an heir to him by the widow. When there was no brother, this duty extended to the next of kin.

Naomi told Ruth that Boaz was going to the threshing floor to winnow barley, and she was to go to him, but first she must prepare herself. A threshing floor is a place of separation—a place where the good grain is separated from the chaff.

Naomi told Ruth to first wash herself and anoint herself with perfume. Then she was to get dressed for the occasion. After that she was to go to the threshing floor, but to not make herself known to Boaz until he had finished eating and drinking.

It's been said that women in the ancient Middle East, when going to be with their lawful husbands, would through modesty go to the foot of the bed, gently raise the covers, and creep under them up to their place. Ruth was to uncover the feet of Boaz and lie down there until he should discover her presence and tell her what to do. This action of Ruth should be interpreted in light of the customs of that day. This was a way of letting a near kinsman know that he had, not only the right but also the request to proceed with the legal steps necessary for exercising his responsibility. Naomi knew the moral character of Boaz, and could safely advise Ruth. She knew Boaz would follow through with the correct actions.

Boaz knew why Ruth was there. Spreading the skirt over the woman was a symbol of taking her under one's protection or entering into marriage with her. By uncovering his feet and lying down there, Ruth was saying, "Take me for your wife; let your name be called on me, and fulfill your lawful duty to me, for you are my kinsman-redeemer to whom the right of redemption belongs." When marriage was solemnized among the Jews, the man threw his skirt or his robe over the wife and covered her head with it.

Though Boaz was not, in fact, Elimelech's closest kinsman, he desired to take on the responsibility. He took the issue up with the nearest kinsman, who determined that he was unable to fulfill the role of kinsman-redeemer. That role then effectually passed to Boaz. When the closer kinsman gave up his right to buy the land, Boaz said unto the elders and to all the people,

> *Ye are witnesses this day, that I have bought all that was Elimelech's, and all that was Chilion's and Mahlon's, of the hand of Naomi. Moreover, Ruth the Moabitess, the wife of Mahlon, have I purchased to be my wife, to raise up the name of the dead upon his*

*inheritance, that the name of the dead be not cut off from among his brethren, and from the gate of his place: ye are witnesses this day. And all the people that were in the gate, and the elders, said, We are witnesses. The LORD make the woman that is come into thine house like Rachel and like Leah, which two did build the house of Israel: and do thou worthily in Ephratah, and be famous in Bethlehem: and let thy house be like the house of Pharez, whom Tamar bare unto Judah, of the seed which the LORD shall give thee of this young woman.* Ruth 4:9-12

Blessings were pronounced upon Boaz and Ruth. They were invoked to make a fruitful house.

Through this story, God illustrates how the first Adam was cut off (seen in the deaths of Elimelech and his sons). But God raised up a kinsman-redeemer, the second Adam, who came through the line of David. He is called the Seed of the woman, and He is Jesus. He is represented in Ruth's story by Boaz. He redeemed the inheritance of his dead relatives. Without his intervention, the names of his dead relatives would have been lost and their bloodline would have ended. Jesus did the same for man. Christ came to redeem the inheritance of His dead "brother," Adam, and also to take the Gentile wife who was left behind, the Church, to raise up seed to keep the family name alive.

Naomi, in the story, is a type of the Holy Spirit, or one called to help. She told Ruth that Boaz was near kin and could fulfill the duty of the kinsman-redeemer. She instructed Ruth on how to request of Boaz that he perform the part of her husband's near kinsman by purchasing the inheritance of Elimelech and taking her as his wife. Like Naomi, the Holy Spirit, our Helper, has been sent to prepare a Bride for the Kinsman-Redeemer, Jesus Christ. Just as Naomi gave Ruth specific instructions on how to prepare for Boaz, the Holy Spirit directs the Bride of Christ on how to prepare for the coming of Christ.

Ruth married Boaz and became the great-grandmother of King David. God rewarded Ruth with a husband and a son, and Naomi found solace for her grief in her grandson. The child, named Obed, became great grandfather to the founder of the royal line from which Christ came.

From the very beginning, in Genesis, God promised that a Redeemer would come through the Seed of the woman. It was a seed that brought life to earth, and a seed that brought death in the garden, Likewise, it would take a Seed to bring restoration to mankind.

God's plan for the redemption of mankind slowly unfolded. He chose the lineage through which His Son would come to earth as our Kinsman-Redeemer. David, the son of Jesse and the grandson of Obed, would begin the royal line through which Christ would come. David was born in Bethlehem in Judah, and so was Christ. The name *David* in Hebrew means, "Beloved." God said of His Son,

*Thou art my beloved Son; in thee I am well pleased.*
Luke 3:22

# 12 – The Twelve Tribes of Israel

When Jacob named his twelve sons, who would eventually become the twelve tribes of Israel, God was actually speaking prophetically through Jacob. Each of the names of the sons is a declaration of the coming of God's Son, the Seed of the woman, who would bruise Satan's head.

A tribe is a social group comprised of numerous families, clans, or generations having common lineage and in which the absolute patriarchal leadership is by virtue of blood and birth.

As God had promised Abraham, from his seed (through Jacob) would come the Seed of the woman.

Each of these twelve sons had a particular destiny, which was prophesied to him by Jacob. Let's look at each of these tribal leaders.

Reuben was the firstborn of Jacob and Leah. He was of a generous nature, but unbalanced. Out of the positive side of his character, Reuben befriended his brother Joseph and was against Joseph being sold or killed when the rest of the brothers allied against him. Out of the negative side, Reuben lay with his father's concubine, and this was reflected in Jacob's prophecy to Reuben.

> *Reuben, thou art my firstborn, my might, and the beginning of my strength, the excellency of dignity, and the excellency of power: unstable as water, thou shalt not excel; because thou wentest up to thy father's bed; then defiledst thou it: he went up to my couch.*
> Genesis 49:3,4

The name *Reuben* means "a son-a substitute for another child." Christ was manifested in Reuben as the firstfruits, and He was a substitute for his brethren.

The second son born to Jacob and Leah was named *Simeon*, which means, "hearing." Simeon performed a cruel act upon the Shechemites to avenge the seduction of his sister, Dinah.

*Levi* was the third son of Jacob and Leah, and his name means, "joined." He joined his brother Simeon in their act of cruelty at Shechem for the evil done against their sister, Dinah. Together these two brothers deceived the Shechemites and then slaughtered the men and took captive their families. Jacob's prophecy to Simeon and Levi was:

> *Cursed be their anger, for it was fierce; and their wrath, for it was cruel: I will divide them in Jacob, and scatter them in Israel.*
> Genesis 49:7

*Judah* means, "praise." Judah was the fourth son of Jacob and Leah. Jacob pronounced a blessing on Judah:

*Judah, thou art he whom thy brethren shall praise: thy hand shall be in the neck of thine enemies; thy father's children shall bow down before thee. Judah is a lion's whelp: from the prey, my son, thou art gone up: he stooped down, he couched as a lion, and as an old lion; who shall rouse him up? The sceptre shall not depart from Judah, nor a lawgiver from between his feet, until Shiloh come; and unto him shall the gathering of the people be. Binding his foal unto the vine, and his ass's colt unto the choice vine; he washed his garments in wine, and his clothes in the blood of grapes: his eyes shall be red with wine, and his teeth white with milk.*
Genesis 49:8-12

*Dan* means, "judge." Dan was the fifth son of Jacob, born to Bilhah, Rachel's maid. The tribe of Dan was driven into the mountains by the Amorites. Dan became the center of idolatry in Israel. As judges worshiping graven images, the tribesmen of Dan became the epitome of corruption. Jacob's prophecy to Dan was:

*Dan shall judge his people, as one of the tribes of Israel. Dan shall be a serpent by the way, an adder in the path, that biteth the horse heels, so that his rider shall fall backward.* Genesis 49:16,17

Naphtali also was born to Bilhah and was Jacob's sixth son. *Naphtali* means, "wrestling." His prophecy was:

*Naphtali is a hind let loose: he giveth goodly words.*
                                        Genesis 49:21

Jacob's seventh son, Gad, was born to Leah's maid, Zilpah. *Gad* means, "good fortune." Jacob's prophecy to Gad was:

*Gad, a troop shall overcome him: but he shall overcome at the last.*                Genesis 49:19

Asher, the eighth son of Jacob, also was born to Leah's maid, Zilpah. *Asher* means, "happiness." Jacob's prophecy to Asher was:

*Out of Asher his bread shall be fat, and he shall yield royal dainties.*                Genesis 49:20

*Issachar* was Jacob's ninth son and the sixth son of Leah. At his birth, his name meant, "hind laborer," but in time it would come to mean, "he will bring reward." The change would come about because the tribe of Issachar would become servants unto tribute. They worked for marauding tribes for the riches of the crops. Therefore, the prophecy to Issachar was:

*Issachar is a strong ass couching down between two burdens: and he saw that rest was good, and the land that it was pleasant; and bowed his shoulder to bear, and became a servant unto tribute.*
                                        Genesis 49:14-15

Zebulun was the tenth son of Jacob and the sixth son of Leah. The name *Zebulun* means, "dwelling."

*Zebulun shall dwell at the haven of the sea; and he shall be for a haven of ships; and his border shall be unto Zidon.* Genesis 49:13

*Joseph*, the firstborn of Jacob and Rachel, means, "increase." He was the eleventh son of Jacob. Jacob loved Rachel above his other wife, Leah, and his concubines. Therefore, his love for Joseph above all his sons was not a secret.

The brothers of Joseph resented him, and their jealousy intensified when their father gave Joseph a coat of many colors. Joseph told his brothers of his dream of harvest time and their servitude unto him. The brothers became angry at the idea of Joseph reigning over them. It was soon after this that they plotted to kill Joseph. It was Judah's suggestion that Joseph be sold into slavery to the Ishmaelites instead. He was sold for twenty shekels of silver and taken to Egypt as a slave.

Divine providence caused Joseph to be elevated in Egypt's court by Pharaoh. He became the most powerful man in Egypt next to Pharaoh. During Joseph's years in power in Egypt, he saved Egypt from famine with a divine plan. Joseph enjoyed a double inheritance through the blessings of his two sons. Joseph's prophecy was:

*Joseph is a fruitful bough, even a fruitful bough by a well; whose branches run over the wall: the archers have sorely grieved him, and shot at him, and hated him: but his bow abode in strength, and the arms of his hands were made strong by the hands of the mighty God of Jacob; (from thence is the shepherd, the stone of Israel:) even by the God of thy father, who shall help thee; and by the Almighty, who shall bless thee with blessings of heaven above, blessings of the deep that lieth under, blessings of the breasts, and of the womb: the blessings of thy father have prevailed above the blessings of my progenitors unto the utmost bound of the everlasting hills: they shall be on the head of Joseph, and on the crown of the head of him that was separate from his brethren.* Genesis 49:22-26

*Benjamin*, the twelfth son of Jacob and the second son of Rachel, means, "son of the right hand." He was renamed after his dying mother called him *Ben-oni*, meaning, "son of sorrow." Benjamin was precious to Jacob because he had favored Rachel. Jacob did not send him to Egypt for food with his brothers, in order to save him from possible mischief. Benjamin's prophecy was:

*Benjamin shall ravin as a wolf: in the morning he shall devour the prey, and at night he shall divide the spoil.*
Genesis 49:27

These were the twelve tribes of Israel and these were the prophecies their father spoke over them and blessed them. These twelve tribes would become the nation of Israel, God's chosen people, and from Israel would come the Christ as well as the foundation of the Body of Christ.

*The Twelve Tribes of Israel*

The names of the twelve tribes of Israel are prophetic to the tribes but they also have a prophetic message within the meanings of their names. The names of the tribes declared the coming of Jesus as the Redeemer of mankind.

Let's recap the meanings of these names:

*Reuben:* a son, a substitute for another child
*Simeon:* hearing
*Levi:* joined
*Judah:* praise, or may God be praised
*Dan:* judge
*Naphtali:* wrestling
*Gad:* good fortune
*Asher:* happiness
*Issachar:* he will bring reward
*Zebulun:* dwelling
*Joseph:* increase
*Benjamin:* son of the right hand

If we assemble all of these meanings, we can create a description of the prophesied Seed who would one day come to these tribes to redeem them.

Here's our description created from the meanings of the names above:

> A ***Son*** will be given as ***a substitute for another*** who will ***hear*** God, and who will create a ***joining*** with God. He will be ***praised*** above all and will ***dwell*** among us, and ***He will bring reward*** and will ***judge***

the world. ***Good fortune*** and ***happiness*** will come as a result of His ***wrestling*** with evil, and there will be an ***increase*** through this ***Son of the right hand*** of God.

Here we find a description of the coming of Christ, the Head of the Body, the One through whom God and man are reconciled.

The Body of Christ is rooted in the twelve tribes of Israel, and founded by the Cornerstone who is Christ. It is here, in the Body of Christ, that man and God are reconciled because of the work Jesus did on the cross.

Remember the question God posed to Ezekiel that we examined in the beginning of this book?—*"Can these bones live?"* Just as surely as the names of the tribes prophesied the coming of Christ and that prophecy was fulfilled, so too has God fulfilled the words He commanded Ezekiel to speak over the bones. The Body of Christ is the fulfillment of Ezekiel's vision. These bones most certainly do live!